THE BLACK-MAN OF ZINACANTAN

THE TEXAS PAN AMERICAN SERIES

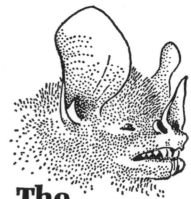

The
Black-man
of
Zinacantan

A CENTRAL AMERICAN LEGEND

*Including an analysis of tales recorded and
translated by Robert M. Laughlin*

By SARAH C. BLAFFER

UNIVERSITY OF TEXAS PRESS
AUSTIN AND LONDON

The Texas Pan American Series is published with the assistance of a revolving publication fund established by the Pan American Sulphur Company and other friends of Latin America in Texas.

F
1221
.T9
H7

Library of Congress Cataloging in Publication Data

Blaffer, Sarah C   1946–
  The Black-man of Zinacantan.

  (Texas Pan American series)
  Bibliography: p.
  1. Tzotzil Indians—Religion and mythology.
2. Zinacantan, Mexico—Social life and customs.
I. Title.
F1221.T9B55   917.2'7   70-185238
ISBN 0-292-70701-0

Composition and printing by The University of Texas Printing Division, Austin
Bound by Universal Bookbindery, Inc., San Antonio

FOR EVON Z. VOGT

who first suggested to me

that *hʔikʼal* might be a bat

CONTENTS

ILLUSTRATIONS

Note about the illustrations: Many of these drawings were taken from Maya and Mexican codices. Some of them represent "abstractions" of the originals; others are more accurate. In order not to suggest that these drawings are suitable for analysis without reference to the originals, the term "adapted" has been used throughout. S.B.

PLATES *following page 80*

MAPS

TABLES

ACKNOWLEDGMENTS

I have been fortunate in having a lot of company, for it would be folly to approach a spook alone. In fact, without the wonderful tales recorded by Robert Laughlin, I could never have met these spooks. Without the guidance of Professor Vogt I would not have known which corners to investigate. It was his suggestion that *hʔikʼal* might be a bat and that someone should look closer at this demon. I hope that this research expresses my appreciation to him for the opportunity to explore these realms. I especially want to thank Francesco Pelizzi for seeing me through the darker moments of this project and Victoria Bricker for pointing out the light and living side of Black-men. Peter Warshall and Bruce Hayward helped me with their wilderness views of bats; Virginia Savage and Joseph Barbieri provided the lively creatures that decorate the text. Thanks go also to Dick Henry who injected a few Kipling characters into the roster of anomalous animals; to Mrs. Titus, who typed all this; to Siri, Kay, and Tess who listened with me one Central American summer for *espantos*; and to Megan.

Robert Laughlin provided much of the material on which this book is based, and, although he had deadlines of his own to meet, he managed to rework translations of some of his tales for publication here. Faithful to the charm and immediacy of the raw material, these new versions trip along so readably that it is hard to believe they represent the ground-breaking work of a man setting down a previously unwritten language. Without the tales themselves there would be little point to publishing this analysis. In addition, Dr. Laughlin's was the most valuable criticism that I encountered. In almost every instance that they were offered, his suggestions have been gratefully pirated. Although I have not met the linguistic standards set in his own work, what consistency and accuracy is achieved for the Tzotzil words used here is totally due to his corrections.

Evon Z. Vogt, Peter Riviere, and Michael Moseley read this analysis when it was first presented as an undergraduate thesis. While I redid the last chapter I benefited from the good advice of Gary Gossen. David Maybury-Lewis was kind enough to take a look at the introduction. The monitoring my thinking underwent from all these people is appreciated.

Among the people whose theories I am indebted to are Mary Douglas and Edmund Leach. Reference to their work should illustrate how deeply they have influenced my orientation. Most importantly, the hypothesis that there is a kind of logic behind myths and that this is a system of thought worth looking into is not a new one; it is scarcely possible to think about myths and their meanings anymore without being influenced by the work of Claude Lévi-Strauss. Though I make few specific references, I hope— if my understanding bears any resemblance to what he meant—my debt to him will be obvious.

THE BLACK-MAN OF ZINACANTAN

i. Introduction

Witches are social equivalents of beetles and spiders
who live in the cracks of the wall and wainscoting.
They attract the fears and dislikes which other am-
biguities and contradictions attract in other thought
structures, and the kind of powers attributed to them
symbolize their ambiguous inarticulate status (Douglas 1966:102).

1. Categories and Anomalies

Mary Douglas suggests that "any culture is a
series of related structures which comprise social forms, values,
cosmology, the whole of knowledge and through which all experience is mediated" (1966:128). If this suggestion is valid, myth
and ritual must reflect the assumptions of the people who devise
them. At the same time, myth and ritual may work to clarify these
assumptions; in the language of Mary Douglas and Victor Turner,
they recreate "prior categories."[1] Claude Lévi-Strauss, the first to

---

[1] "The analysis of ritual cannot begin until we recognize ritual as an attempt to
create and maintain a particular culture, a particular set of assumptions by which
experience is controlled" (Douglas 1966: 128). Religious ritual has a creative
function: "It actually creates or recreates the categories through which men per-
ceive reality—the axioms underlying the structure of society and the laws of the
natural or moral orders" (Turner 1968: 7).

apply the structural approach to a large corpus of myths, speaks of cracking a "code." The cipher he is after is the product of the mind of man ordering his perception of the world he lives in.

One convenient solution to the problem of simplifying experience is to set up oppositions or contrasting categories: experience falls into binary classifications. Perhaps it is the success of this kind of mental adaptation that is attested to by frequent similarities found in myths and rituals from different parts of the world. There are only a limited number of meaningful oppositions relevant to man's perceptions of the natural and social world.

Once such a system of categories is set up, a great deal of energy is expended in maintaining it. According to Douglas, we have a built-in "filtering mechanism."

As . . . experiences pile up, we make a greater investment in our system of labels . . . It gives us confidence. At any given time we may have to modify our structure of assumptions to accommodate new experience, but the more consistent experience is with the past, the more confidence we have in our assumptions. Uncomfortable facts which refuse to be fitted in, we find ourselves ignoring or distorting so that they do not disturb these established assumptions. By and large anything we take note of is pre-selected and organized in the very act of perceiving (Douglas 1966:36–37).

Nevertheless, any system of classification that is at all ambitious is bound to give rise to anomalies, and a culture must confront this eventuality. A culture that fails to come to terms with anomalies risks forfeiting confidence in the system.

The first step in dealing with anomalies is to recognize them as such and to put them into a special category. When something is classified as "anomalous," it is labeled as a peculiar kind of event. The semblance of order is restored. Doubts about the culturally dictated categories are erased, and, in addition, the categories of which the anomaly is *not* a member are clarified (Douglas 1966: 38–39).

Uncommon or ambiguous eventualities, moments "in and out of time,"[2] animals or substances that belong to one classification

---

[2] Victor Turner quotes this phrase from T. S. Eliot. Turner originally applied it

but could easily belong to another—all of these could qualify as "anomalous." People could also qualify. Humans who behave strangely, who disobey or ignore a society's accepted conventions present a social problem, but they also threaten certain premises held by those around them. If humans are supposed to behave in a certain way, are people who behave "like animals" still considered human?

In our society we might describe such behavior as "perverted," and classify such people as "misfits." The Ndembu people of Central Africa have a special word for this problem, *Ku-shumana*, which means "to behave unnaturally." "If a father were to eat his own children, if a child were to order an elder about, or if an animal were to dress in clothes, these things would be *Ku-shumana*" (Turner 1967:205). These terms have also to do with transgressed norms. If they are applied disapprovingly, it may be because such behavior threatens to undermine a culture's classification of what behavior is "civilized" and "human."

In some societies, people who behave perversely are witches. They are a bit removed from what is human, a little too close to nature. They behave "like animals" and are associated with them. Beidelman describes such a class of beings as it occurs among the Kaguru of Africa. The Kaguru tend to interpret most anti-social behavior, especially the failure to meet obligations towards kin, as witchcraft. A witch is said to work at night, to be incestuous, to delight in injuring others, to devour human beings, and to travel in the air clinging to a hyena. The witch epitomizes departure from that society's rules of human conduct (Beidelman 1963:68), and yet it is clear that this figure is not entirely inhuman either. A special classification is in order. Though the term *anomalous* means "abnormal," relative to the categories dictated by a given culture, these anomalies can be abstracted from specific cultures and compared. Misfits, witches, and people who are *Ku-shumana* all have something in common.

---

to ritual time but perhaps would be happy to see this phrase turned to describe any period where humans experience the supernatural.

2. A Set of Anomalies

In this analysis I will be discussing a legendary Maya demon, the *hʔikʼal*, as he is represented by the Tzotzil speakers of Zinacantan. Although I will be most concerned with the current manifestations of this spook[3] in myth and ritual, I will also diagram the associations that *hʔikʼal* holds in common with an ancient Maya demon and draw comparisons between *hʔikʼal* and other spooks in the Maya area that the Maya of Zinacantan may never have heard of. In part I am basing these treatments on the kind of relationship that exists between an American misfit, a Kaguru witch, and a person who is *Ku-shumana*; in terms of the dictated categories of the specific cultures, each of these characters is anomalous.

I am also basing my analysis on the assumption that a genetic relationship exists between all the Maya speakers in the not-too-distant past (Vogt 1964). Though Maya mythologies and Maya attitudes toward spooks have undoubtedly changed and though some elements must by now be dialect-specific, I suspect that many categories based on ancient models have been retained. Such retention would follow from the flexibility of the category in which people store "anomalous" experience and from the tendency for unwieldly data to be distorted—rather than for categories to be changed. To the extent that I draw on history, mine is an adulterated, not a pure, structural approach.

In this paper I will draw comparisons between *hʔikʼal* and a potpourri of other spooks taken from Maya peoples west and south of the Tzotzil and from other municipios in Highland Chiapas. By definition these creatures evade classification, and it is far easier to describe what they are not than what they are. A spook is neither alive nor dead, man nor animal. It may seem like the one and act like the other, or else appear and act the role in full; still, it is never entirely anything except ambiguous. Whether a spook actually takes on animal form, or whether it simply behaves like an animal, at

---

[3] In Spanish American parlance *espanto* means something that frightens people; this is a convenient term for me to use and I translate it as "spook."

some stage in its career a spook conducts itself in a manner that no true human would.

In the Maya area these spooks fit into a framework constructed for anomalies. Within this classification, they are connected with all kinds of other anomalies. No less ambiguous than a spook's identity are the localities they inhabit. They live in caves, or just below the surface of rivers, in strange places that are hard to categorize as air or ground, above the earth or beneath the earth. They wander in the transition zones between one thing and another. They frequent corners and crossroads—places that lead in several directions and in no direction—and they may be found in cemeteries, where the world of the living meets that of the dead. People, especially travelers, who are themselves in transition between one place and another, come across them on mountain paths or in the area just outside the village that is neither inhabited nor wild. Spooks are associated with doorways and eaves, where they are neither in the house nor outside of it.

Theirs are the midnight and the twilight hours between night and day, and they are especially dangerous to those who are likewise in tension zones between two states—the sick, the insane, people who are asleep or drunk, those who are not completely alive (or conscious) but who are also not yet dead.

Beliefs about *espantos* play on these contrasts between the living and the dead, between men and animals, nature and culture. Like the dead, a charcoal-cruncher (Zinacantan) may have cold limbs or a cold face. The *yalen beket* of San Pedro Chenalhó removes its flesh and wanders as a skeleton. Some spooks (like *xtabai* in Yucatán or *špak'in te?* in Zinacantan) putrefy, turning into rotten wood or excrement once they are exposed. Others, like the *brujos* of Yucatán and Belize, remove their skin or just send part of their body (only the head of the charcoal-cruncher goes) off into the night. Sometimes this segmented head attaches itself to an animal. In other cases the spook becomes an animal.

Usually the animals spooks turn into are themselves anomalous. They are often domestic animals like pigs and goats and dogs who are seen living in close proximity to men and yet are not men. These are animals who eat human refuse—especially dogs who have a

reputation for eating excrement.[4] The *güin* (or *win*) and the *cadejo*
(northwestern Guatemala) almost invariably turn into "shaggy
dogs"; the *characotel* is frequently a goat.

The *characoteles* wear chains or bells or corncobs about their
necks, perhaps to emphasize that though they are "wild" they still
belong to the cultural world of which they are a function. The
ambiguity is between a domestic animal that serves man and a wild
run-away thing that plagues him.

Even those spooks not specifically identified with animals partake
of an animal or abnormal diet. Like corpse-eater (Zinacantan),
they feed on raw flesh, especially human carrion. Like *el win*
(Santiago El Palmar), they gnaw on the bones of dead people.
Spooks are associated with excrement and waste. The charcoal-
cruncher, a spook notorious in Zinacantan, is particularly interesting; this spook eats charcoal, a "dead" substance, which, however,
is also "cooked" and associated with cooking, the "civilizing"
process for human foods. Such distinctions as these between nature
and culture become especially significant when destroying a spook
or "civilizing" it. To destroy a spook one throws salt (a substance
used in cooking) or garlic (used in curing) on it. To punish it,
one beats it with whips as though one were taming an animal. The
treatment dealt to spooks will be discussed in chapter 5.

Whether or not a spook actually turns into an animal, it behaves
like one. Spooks are anti-social, and they ignore or else reverse the
accepted rule of human behavior. They are adulterers, sodomites,
thieves, and murderers. They kidnap, lead people astray, carry sickness, practice incest, and eat human flesh. Even those spooks which
are only part-time and which have two identities can be recognized
while in human form. They behave strangely or else suffer from
some physical deformity or peculiar aspect. The first thing that the
husband of a corpse-eater (Zinacantan) is likely to notice is that
she will not speak to him or join the family at meals; she becomes
divorced from normal social activities. Before changing shape (into
an animal), it is customary for a witch to do a flip or to roll around
on the ground. *Characoteles* go about pinching the noses of their

[4] In Zinacantan, at least, dogs really do eat "shit and tortillas" (Acheson
1962–1963)—a strange blend of animal and human diet!

sleeping husbands and children. To make certain that no one is awake, a *characotel* may stick her rear into her husband's face. In human form, these spooks may be recognized by a bad smell, blood-shot eyes, or protruding canines, or by having "letters no one can read" on the skin of their torsos (*el win* in Santiago El Palmar).

The criteria then for being a spook involve form and attributes, habitat, diet, and behavior; the creature will usually be anomalous on each count. Though it may be risky to list specific categories—neither man nor animal, neither dead nor alive, neither one place nor another—that determine "spookhood" among Maya peoples, comparisons of their tales indicate that such a listing may be feasible. My approach will be to set up opposing categories and define the spooks by their intermediate position between two poles.

In chapter 5, these oppositions are elaborated and made more specific to *hʔikʼal* and to Tzotzil beliefs. Chapter 6 suggests a third set of oppositions, that between male and female. But, at this point all I need to point out are the analogies that seem to exist between these spooks, their actions, and their qualities. All these anomalous creatures, conditions, and places are interrelated. A kind of equivalence exists between the themes and details of the stories of one

Table 1. Categories Based on Opposition between Nature and Culture

	Culture	In-between	Nature
Form and attributes	human	human in animal form or with animal attributes	animal
	tame	a domestic creature gone wild	wild
Habitat	settled areas or inside house	the edge of village, path, doorways, etc.	wild places or outside house
Behavior	in accordance with human norms	ignoring or reversing norms	not aware of proper ways of doing things
Diet	human food, which is cooked	human-like creature eating carrion or waste, which may be cooked	animal food (carrion and waste), which is raw

Table 2. Categories Based on Opposition between Being Alive and Being Dead

	Alive	*In-between*	*Dead*
Form and *attributes*	flesh warm body	skeleton-person cold limbs	fleshless cold body
*Condition**	healthy flesh	putrefied flesh	bare skeleton
	conscious	unconscious (drunk, asleep, sick, insane, etc.)	dead
	being born	born dead or with a veil	not being born
Habitat	in the house	in the cemetery	buried
Diet	food	doesn't eat	nothing

* this point will be elaborated in chapter 5; it applies also to the spooks' victims

spook and those of another. A more detailed justification for this view can be found in the following charts and in those in Appendix II.

Readers unfamiliar with Maya demonology might begin with Appendix II: "Legions of Shadow-makers." For those who find the early chapters overloaded with documentation, the main points of my analysis are summarized in chapters VI and VII.

The tables are set up as a convenience to the reader so that he can compare some of the recurring elements in the various spook identities. The format is flexible, but in general self-explanatory. If my information comes from data recorded for a particular location, the name of that village appears in italics in the lefthand column. Otherwise, I have merely listed the source or the dialect group. References for these descriptions are listed in Appendix I.

Table 3. *Characotel* (For sources see Appendix I)

	Animal Form	Attributes	Behavior (functions or idiosyncracies)	Habitat (where or when it is likely to be encountered)	Treatment (to destroy it or drive it away)
San Pedro la Laguna (Paul)	Burro Ass Cat Dog Pig (white) Sheep	Wears chain, bell, or corncob around neck Leader wears bell Bad smell like buzzard Born with veil	Pinches nose of husband Puts rear in husband's mouth Puts skirt over husband Steps over husband 4 times	Corners Lake Atitlán	Beat it with sticks of chichicaste
(Rosales)	A *Q'i'som*,[1] or may remain as woman				
Agua Escondida	Dog Goat (same as *cadejo*)	Shaggy coat A dark dog with red eyes Hooves Drags a piece of chain	Takes hat off to others	Cemetery	
Panajacbel	Sheep Dog "Carnero-Woman"	Face of a dog	Pinches nose of husband and children		Husband steals clothes and applies salt
Santa Lucia Uxtatlán	Dog Sheep Billy-Goat (same as Güin)	Born with a veil	Takes care of drunks	Roadside crosses	
Samayac	"An animal" (same as *cadejo*)		Takes care of drunks		

[1] a *Q'i'som* is any transformed animal

Table 4. *Charcoal-cruncher*

	Attributes	Behavior	Habitat	Treatment	Diet
Zinacantan					
RML 12	Wife removes head at night	Her head attaches to husband; to deer (while in woods)		Salt, garlic, tobacco put on flesh	Charcoal
RML 47	Wife's head goes off at night	Sends sickness; frightens people	Eaves Fireside	Hot water is thrown on it; salt is put on its flesh	Charcoal
RML 60	Wife's head goes off at night	Head attaches to man; attaches to deer (while man is in pine tree)		Hot water is thrown on it; salt is put on severed neck	Charcoal
RML 81	Man's head goes off at night (his face is ugly and cold)	Head lands on top of child	Top of wall	Salt on severed neck	Charcoal
VRB 106		Head sticks to husband while he is in woods searching for pine cones		Salt on neck	Charcoal Starves to death

Table 5. *Cadejo*

	Animal Form	*Attributes*	*Behavior*	*Habitat*
Agua Escondida	Dog (same as *charcotel*)	Shaggy coat Hooves Chain		Only at night
Santa Lucía Uxtatlán	Dog	Wears cross on forehead	Takes care of drunks	
Santo Tomás Chichicastenango	(Span. *xalbai*)	(To pass over it means death in a week; must make sign of cross with left hand)		
Asturias' Mulata	"Sisimite's dog-lion-tiger-tapir-calf"	Faithful Bloodthirsty Mane Horns Hooves "With the skin of a hairy river"		
Among the *Chorti*	Dog Tiger	Long plaited hair Very fleet of foot		Lives high in hill, rocky precipices
Samayac	Dog (like *charcotel*)		Takes care of drunks	

Table 6. *Güin* (or *Win*)

	Animal Form	Attributes	Behavior	Habitat	Diet
Santiago el Palmar	Any animal or bird met at night, esp. dogs	Unusually ugly blazing red eyes; cross or letters no one can read on torso	Steals chickens	Cemetery	Eats bones of dead
Santa Lucía Uxtatlán	An animal ("this is not here, but on coast")	Tail	Steals chickens	Cemetery	
Samayac	An animal		Leaves clothes at cross	Cemetery	
Finca Ascensión	Dog				
Nebaj	An animal		Kills chickens		

Table 7. *X'pakinte* (*Spak'in te?*)

	Attributes	Behavior	Habitat
Cancuc	Only the head changes	Uses voice to lead people astray into canyons	
Chamula	Dresses up like a woman	Plays with men who walk in roads; causes men to become lost in middle of forest	Roads
Zinacantan	Impersonates victim's wife	Appears to drunks	
	Back of head hollow		
	Hair of poisonous caterpillars	Shows her sexual parts to men, but they are only excrement	

	Attributes	Behavior	Location
San Antonio, Belize (Kekchi Maya)	Impersonates sweetheart	Walks backwards to disguise her hollow back	Forest on the edge of village
	Hollow, rough back	Turns into rotten wood	

Table 8. *Siguamaba*

	Attributes	Behavior
Santa Lucia Uxtatlán	Beautiful Woman—impersonator of loved one	Leads people astray in canyons
	Long hair	
Asturias' Mulata	"Warrior woman of solitary canyons"	Looks for drunkards
	"Weeping water hair"	
Chorti	Impersonates sweethearts	Molests immoral people, especially drunks
	Wears cloth around face	A meeting always results in insanity; carries off children and returns them three days later, insane

Table 9. *Brujas*

	Animal Form	Behavior	Diet	Habitat	Treatment
Zinacantan	Domestic: Cow Cat Goat Pig Horse Wild: Fox Skunk Coyote Jaguar	Brings illness and death	Eats corpses	Cemetery	
San Antonio, *Belize* (Kekochi)	Mule Owl	Removes head and throws self on ground (every Friday at mid- night)			Ashes are put on it.
Santa Lucia *Uxtalán*	"Bruja coche" Pig		Eats Bats		
Yucatán (Castillo)		Removes skin Repeats strange utterances at mid- night		Clearing in woods	Salt put on discarded skin

Table 10. "White-Bundle"

	Attributes	Behavior	Habitat
Zinacantan	A person in form of white bundle	Goes around sick people Passes cross and throws garlic Takes off clothes and rolls Crawls on 4 legs If a person is very sick, throws on more sickness	Arrives in wind At crosses
Lab	("El Shulucchan") Size of a horse ("Tonilna") Horns Like a rat Squirrel Billy goat Wildcat Buzzard Cat Nagual	Comes around sick people Throws out illness	In laguna of cerro grande; seen only if there is current; comes around bed

Table 11. *Buzzard Man and Lechuza*

	Animal Form	Attributes	Behavior
Zinacantan	K'us Cukutin, a hot country bird (Red-billed pigeon)	Lazy man Unfaithful	When his relations see he is bad, they turn him into a bird
	Buzzard ("Xulem Vinik")	Lazy Robber	When his wife finds out, she drives the bird-man out of the house
	Buzzard	Lazy	Burns himself in a fire looking for a meal of carrion
	Buzzard	Lazy Robber Buzzard-turned-man stinks	Burns himself in fire looking for a meal of carrion
Panajacbel	Buzzard	Lazy	
San Pedro la Laguna	Buzzard	Wife discovers him by his bad smell	
San Pedro Chenalbó	Buzzard	Lazy Stinks	Feeds on carrion
San Pedro la Laguna		(A child who urinates in its clothes is told it smells like a buzzard; also 'men who do not wash feet)	
Chinautla	Owl	A charmed person, an invisible thief	
San Andrés Tuxtla	Lechuza, tecolote, or brujo, which changes into an animal connected with owl	Can be heard whistling as he flies through night	
Finca Ascensión	A big bird (like the characotel)		

ii. The Culprit

The Spook (*h²ik'al*)

Well, once there were many spooks. The women's husbands weren't around. They had gone to the lowlands (to farm). Now it seems they slept at dusk. "Let's sleep. Comadre, will you listen for me (and tell me) if my corn boils over?"

"All right, comadre, maybe I'll hear it."

"I won't know because I am going to sleep at the fireside," said the person whose corn boiled over.

"All right, maybe I'll hear it," said her comadre. She hears it hissing now. "Comadre, comadre, your corn is boiling over," she said.

But it was the woman's blood now. The spook was there already. "The corn is ready, comadre," said the spook (Robert M. Laughlin, tale 122).

I n the Tzotzil world of Zinacantan there are two kinds of Black-men, the black-skinned trickster of the myths and the human impersonator of this demon who figures in ritual. Both manifestations of this spook are called *h²ik'al* (plural *h²ik'aletik*) and refer to the same ideal type, a winged[1] black demon with

---

[1] In the myths, *h²ik'al* has wings attached to his feet; in conversations about the ritual impersonators of this demon, Zinacantecos describe the performers as wearing black capes representing wings. Their costumes may, however, be different—ladino style clothes and leather outfits.

a sinister reputation for unrestrained sexuality, people-snatching, and cannibalism.

1. *H°ik'al* in Myth

Most of my information about *h°ik'al* comes from the fieldnotes of Victoria R. Bricker and Professor E. Z. Vogt and from myths about the Black-man collected and translated by Robert M. Laughlin. These sources will be referred to by the initials of the recorder, VRB, EZV, RML, and by the index number as it appears in their notes. The number of references that I will need to make indicates the extent of my debt to these people, and to the Harvard Chiapas-Project files. Without the availability of theirs and other unpublished material about Chiapas, and without their generous help, I could never have attempted this analysis of *h°ik'al*.

H°ik'al, as he is described in myth and in conversations with Tzotzil informants, is a small, black-skinned, curly haired creature who wears wings or some other flying device on his feet.[2] He lives in caves and comes out at dusk to steal chickens and to molest people. A thief and a murderer, he also carries lone women off to his cave and keeps them there. *H°ik'al*'s most striking feature is his sexuality; he has a six-foot-long, death-dealing penis. Women raped by Black-man become superimpregnated. In some cases the woman swells up and dies; in others, her children begin to appear within three days of conception and then keep coming, one child a night. A common complaint concerning *h°ik'aletik* is that they "breed too fast." Despite this potency, Zinacantecos are convinced that there used to be many more Black-men than there are today. Formerly, they could not leave their houses for fear of Black-men. One Zinacanteco narrates: "The spooks have gotten fewer. Long ago we couldn't go outside until nine o'clock. At three o'clock you close up the house, close the door . . . Supplies of wood and water must be stored ahead of time; all needs must be attended to inside the house."

---

[2] In Field Interview-8 between E. Z. Vogt and Domingo de la Torre Perez, Domingo specifically says that what *h°ik'al* wears are *not* wings but "something behind his feet which permitted him to fly."

The purpose of this analysis will be to explore the logic behind the scenes depicted in the Black-man myths. Although I will be drawing on archaeological and ethnographic data and on descriptions of *hʔikʼal* in ritual, the focus of my discussion will be the tales themselves, and it would be helpful if the reader had some plot background as well as a feel for the Tzotzil narratives. One problem with oral narrative is the frequent recurrence of the same patterns, combined in various ways. For literate people, with a different tradition of storytelling, these transcriptions can make hard reading. Within the same version, the victim who is kidnapped may be a person already murdered. Or, as with a nine-lived cat, Black-man may suffer what seems like multiple deaths in the course of one myth. Sometimes the narrator clarifies that it is the children of *hʔikʼal* that still need killing, but other times the same demon will be both shot to death and burned (RML, tale 71) or stabbed and hanged (RML, tale 123). This repetition is especially evident in the longer tales. Often what seems like parts of other situations are tacked on.

This overlap makes it difficult to classify the tales. Nevertheless, as a convenience to the reader, I will attempt to divide them at this point into three groups in which the narratives describe similar situations. A fourth, miscellaneous group, will deal with "tacked-on" portions from other tales. All the tales mentioned appear in this chapter as rubrics or in Appendix III. Outlines of the tales can be found in chapter 6.

In general, the Black-man tales describe one of three situations:

(1) (RML, tales 23, 67, 71, and 122)
Hʔikʼal comes to the house of a woman cooking corn and murders her or carries her off, or both. He grabs her while she is asleep by the fire or when she goes to pour out the *nixtamal*.[3] Each time, the woman's neighbor hears the corn boiling over onto the fire, making the sound *pululu*; actually, this sound is the blood of *hʔikʼal*'s victim.

2. (RML, tales 123, 124, 126, and 127; EZV, Field Interview-8)
Hʔikʼal accosts either a man alone or two travelers, and they fight.

---

[3] *Nixtamal* is lime water in which the corn is boiled before it is ground.

Except in one case (tale 124) the men are unconscious, asleep, drunk, or in a faint. The outcome will be the death of *hʔikʔal* and either a trip to Black-man's home or the rescue of one of his victims.

3. (RML, tales 68 and 130)

Hʔikʔal longs for company and beseeches Saint Sebastian the Martyr and San Lorenzo to give him one of their children. These tales describe his quest. The fact that the saints do not really give him one of their children suggests that pious people who comply with Zinacanteco norms are protected from *hʔikʔal*. This point will be elaborated later.

In seven of the eleven tales, there is some reference to Black-man murdering or carrying off a woman. The exceptions are RML, tales 124, 125, 127, and EZV, Field Interview-8. In tale 127, Black-man attempts to carry off first a drunken man, then a small boy. He also raids a chicken house. In tales 124 and 125 and in Field Interview-8, a traveler defeats Black-man and then flies off to Black-man's home. In tale 124, the man tricks *hʔikʔal*'s mother into giving him dried meat; in this tale and in the interview, Black-man is made to give the man money. Although I cannot do much with the second batch of exceptions, carrying off the animals that are food for humans (tale 127) may be a substitute for raping a woman, who is food for such animallike creatures as Black-man.[4]

With this emphasis on the molesting of women, it is not surprising that rescue from rape is the most prevalent theme of the "tacked-on" tales. These episodes do not stand by themselves; instead, they compose a fourth situation occurring in conjunction with one of the other three.

4. In two tales (RML, tales 123 and 126) the travelers rescue a girl wrapped up in a straw mat. Elsewhere (RML, tales 71 and 130), the girl who is stolen while throwing out her *nixtamal* or

---

[4] At the fiesta of San Sebastian the *hʔikʔaletik* dance with roosters "to show" that they are chicken thieves. Looking at an earlier translation of tale 127 in which *hʔikʔal* "embraced" the chickens, Vogt and I discussed the possibility that *hʔikʔal*'s relation with the chickens might have sexual overtones. The newer and more accurate translation, "picking up" the chickens, makes this interpretation questionable.

while kneading clay is rescued from the spook's cave by being pulled out with a rope.

Certain general trends begin to emerge from these tales. Whereas women tend to be punished—raped or murdered—men in these tales, the brave ones at least, are rewarded with money, meals, or marriage. Some of the tales (RML, tales 67 and 122) explicitly begin "just women"; when men are involved, discussions of bravery and cowardice, proper and improper reactions crop up.

No one version can be considered typical, nor can any tale be labeled "prior" to, or more complete than, another; in order to keep this chapter reasonably short, however, only one tale representative of each situation will be included here. I hope that the tales in the appendix will also be read and compared. The following story is a fairly long example of *hʔikʼal*'s murdering a woman who falls alseep by her cooking fire. Despite the welter of fatalities here—*hʔikʼal* is scalded, he is skewered and roasted, he is burned—the outcome should be clear, that, somehow, *hʔikʼal* is cooked.

THE SPOOK (*hʔikʼal*)[5]

Once there were a great many spooks [*hʔikʼaletik*]. Because of the spooks, it wasn't possible to walk around. You couldn't go outside until nine o'clock. You couldn't go out alone. We walked with escorts. Then the women got smart.

There was [a woman] who had a comadre. They were neighbors. "Please, comadre, wake me up, because I'm cooking my little bit of corn," she said.

"All right," answered her comadre. "Comadre, comadre," she said. [The other's] corn was spilling suddenly in the middle of the fire. But no, it wasn't corn putting out the fire. It was because the spook went and grabbed, molested the woman. The disgusting spook's penis was so long it killed the woman. The woman died. When the other woman woke up, it was just blood there hissing.

You see her other friends came in a group. They came to look at their comadre. But you see she was already dead. As for that spook he was caught on an upright stake at the door. He was impaled. That house post came out of his mouth. And then they put him over the fire. They

---

[5] Whereas I use "spook" as a general term, Laughlin uses it for the creature I call Black-man.

cooked him so that he would die for good. They boiled hot water for him, so that they could scald him like a chicken.

You see that one died like that. He burned up. They gathered firewood for him. They [used] corncobs, since the people of long ago had a lot of corn. They didn't throw out their corncobs. They were glad to use them as firewood it seems. One died, but that wasn't enough, since there were so very many spooks then. Hairy Hand was the name of that spook who died that way. Hairy Hand had many many children left—other spooks.

There was a lady, that comadre. She was clever. You see she boiled hot water. She put the boiling water on top of the fire. He entered. "Nanita, are you here," he said as he arrived.

"I'm here. Come in. Do you drink coffee, do you drink *posol*? We'll boil the water for it," he was told.

"I do," said the spook. He drank the *posol*. He ate the *posol*. When he was touching it to his mouth, they scalded him with boiling water. But you know he wasn't burned well enough until he threw down his gourd. Then she threw it. The boiling water was thrown at his head. Then he died.

That comadre won. That was the way she threw boiling water at him. She scalded him it seems.

That one died. He died because of them. They put him on the fire. He burned up. The woman's comadre, that lady's comadre, said to them: "Come on, let's burn them up. That's how we'll get rid of the spooks. They grab people so much now. It isn't right the way they molest us. It isn't right what happened to that other woman. What he did—he dragged her to his cave."

They breed too fast. One child a night. How could we win? Some hunters passed by behind the cave. There where the cave was. The hunters passed by. "What men are you? Take me out. Come, take me away."

"We can't take you away now because we haven't anything to get you out with. The cave is too deep. I'll come to hunt and I'll bring my lasso to get you out," replied the hunters. They went to hunt on purpose there where she was. They took their rope. They threw it down. "I've come. Come out! It's me whom you told to get you out," said the men.

The woman came out. Her children were lined up along the hem of her skirt. They grabbed the hem of her skirt. One after another stuck on. One of her little children came out. With difficulty she finished pulling off the others. Six of that woman's children stayed behind it seems.

Now the one that came out sticking to her skirt was already walking. It was following right behind. It went to the house of that woman. They looked for four staves when they arrived at her house, when they arrived to return that woman at the house of her father and mother, it seems. There where she went out she had been pouring out the lime water when she was stolen away long ago.

They arrived there. They looked for those four staves. They held a curing ceremony. She had a curing ceremony. Her candles were offered [at the shrines], but it did no good. That spook went there three nights searching. He just wanted to steal his wife back. But that child of his, the little baby spook, they stuck in the fire so he would die. As for that old spook, this is what they did about him—those four staves at the edge of her bed guarded her. They guard people. He never could take the woman away. But you see, I don't know if the woman lasted one month or three weeks. She died. The woman just urinated lime water. She had diarrhea. That's how the woman died when she returned it seems.

They buried her. The spook kept coming all the time, frightening people. He thought his wife was still there. When he returned it seems she had died already. She had already been buried. The woman had entered the grave. The spook hadn't wanted his wife to die. He thought she was still alive. He wanted to take her to his house another time.

The people were scared. They were upset about him wandering and wandering about, coming to look and look [for his wife]. They just assembled to get him. Four men gathered together at night. They shot at him, they just shot at him, but they never hit him. It wasn't until they went to look in that cave that the woman had been taken out of. They went to kill him with guns. He died, the old one died.

But his children were left. So then the women assembled to get them. They died of boiling water. They burned them. They would cook a turkey for them. Now they don't finish eating their turkey. First the spooks are scalded to death with boiling water. Or else, when the hot water is bubbling, when the water is boiling, then they scald the spooks first. Or else when their meal is bubbling—"Wait, drink a little coffee," they would say. Then when he touched the gourd to his lips they would throw the boiling water at him and scald him. That's how they killed them. They cut them to pieces with machetes so that their flesh wouldn't stick together. [The people] called them Hairy Hands long ago. They couldn't be killed unless they were scalded with boiling water. That's how they got rid of the spooks long ago.

You see that's how the spooks have gotten fewer. Long ago we

couldn't go outside until nine o'clock. At three o'clock you close up the
house, close the door. You'd better have your water, your things [in-
side]. A load of firewood is put inside during the day, no more can
come in. Then we draw our water. We can't go anywhere. The house is
closed. Someplace inside you go to the bathroom. Look for a place to go
to the bathroom. We can't go outside. We were closed up inside long
ago. My mother told about it. It seems it was my mother's grandmother
who saw it. But now there aren't any. God willing there aren't any
spooks now. There's nothing to scare people, because they were scalded
to death with boiling water. They were burnt up. Long ago the fires
were made for them.

It was her comadre who spoke to her. "Comadre, what is it, what is
it, your corn boiled over. Look!"

But it wasn't her comadre who answered, it was the spook now. "The
corn's ready, comadre, the corn's ready, comadre," the spook answered.

They went to look. What do you think? It was the spook they found.
The spook fled, but he was caught on a stake by the door. His ass was
impaled. It came out his mouth. They burned him up (RML, tale 71).

The next myth combines a version of *hʔik'al* accosting travelers
with a tale of rescue.

THE SPOOK (*Hʔik'al*) AND THE GIRL FROM MAGDALENAS

Once the spook, well, he had a fight with the Zinacantecs. Two of
them slept in a cave.

"Oh, I don't know why I'm afraid. Man, if something should come,"
said one of them.

"What are you scared of? What the hell, are you blue-assed [do you
wear women's skirts]?" said the other.

"Hell, but I don't know. You be brave!"

"I am brave, man. Put a lot of firewood on. Good. Are you blue-
assed? What are you scared of man?" he said. [The other] was very
scared. He was chilled.

Oh, late at night the spook came whooshing down. He saw the fire
gleaming in the cave. There is a field there. He set down his pack there.

He went in to talk to them. Oh, hell, as for the brave man, his ass was
sopping wet now. He had pissed on himself.

To the man who [first] had been scared—"What's up, friend? What
are you doing?"

"Sir, I'm not doing anything."

"I'll warm myself."

"Fine, warm yourself, sir," he said.

"Do you want a smoke?" [the spook] said.

"I'll smoke," [the man] replied. He was given a cigarette. He crumbled it up like this. He just wasted it. He crumbled it up this way. "Bastard, what are you doing to your cigarette? Hell, I haven't finished one," [the spook] said.

"Well, sir, I'm smoking the way I always smoke. Hell, I'll smoke," he said. Well, [the spook] gave him another. Three cigarettes he took.

"Bastard, this kind of act is no good. Bastard, you'll see. Do you want to fight?"

"Well, fight if you know how to fight, sir, but me, I don't know how to fight. I'm just sitting here warming myself," he said. The bastard [the Zinacantec] had a good stick. What a man!

Well, you see, "You bastard," said [the spook].

"Look here, whose bastard? Hell, I'm not your bastard, because your hair is so kinky, you bastard," said the man.

"Well, wait, I'll draw a line." [The spook] drew the line. It was made now. "Well, stand here," said [the spook].

"Fine," he replied.

[The spook] rose up. He had a sword. He thrust it point downwards like this. But it fell on the ground. The man whacked him two, three times, right off when he rose up. Well, you see, he came down. He grew weaker and weaker. Now he rose up only a short distance. [The man] hit his legs. He was the same distance as a bird. He came down to the ground.

But the brave man's piss was just pouring out. Oh, nothing could be done, the bastard's filth ran out.

Then he died. The horrible spook just had his teeth bared. The spook's teeth were bared. He died. [The man] tied his neck. With a lasso he tied it. Turning blue [in the face, the spook] died. He was tied. He just turned blue.

You see, [the man] went to look where [the spook] had left, where he had left . . . There rolled up in a new straw mat was a girl from Magdalenas. "Bastard, what kind of thing are you? Are you a spook?"

"It's me, sir. Don't kill me. Untie me," she said.

He untied her. Now a wife had come to the man. The girl was a lush babe. He married her. He didn't return her. "Well, but what happened to you?" he said. Now that he had a wife, the Magdalenas girl sitting there, he was swishing a switch, but the ["brave" Zinacantec] got a good beating.

"Never mind, if it's just a whipping, don't kill me. Take her. I thought I was brave. I wasn't brave at all," he said.

A Magdalenas girl. "Hell, it [must be] a Magdalenas man coming," said the men who had stayed behind. "But how did the bastard do it?" said the men. "He wasn't afraid. She's a devil. She has taken the devil's orders" (RML, tale 123).

Interesting dichotomies are set up in this tale between those responses which are proper for men and those which are not. A distinction is made between the Zinacanteco who is "manly" and the one who is afraid. The brave man asks his companion, "Are you a woman?" These issues, involving ultimately what it is to be a "man" in Zinacantan, will be discussed in chapter 6. *H'ik'al* also exhibits behavior that, by human standards, is abnormal. He is the kind of creature who bares his teeth and probably never prayed the vespers (RML, tale 124). *H'ik'al* does *not* behave as any proper human would; by default, he is behaving like an animal and is associated with natural and supernatural realms. *H'ik'al* shares his habitat of caves with animals like the jaguar and with ancestor spirits in the form of lightning and whirlwind (Stubblefield 1961:5). A further connection between *h'ik'al* and the supernatural is suggested by his cold hands, a characteristic of the dead.

Some of the strangest descriptions of *h'ik'al* involve mistaken identities, whereby he is actually confused with an animal. A young girl about to be kidnapped watches him land. "She thought it was a buzzard standing there" (see tale 130 below). An informant who dreamed about the Black-man related the following: "There was a horrible big buzzard there. It went chasing after me. But now it didn't look like a buzzard. It was a horrible person" (RML, dream 190). In another story, *h'ik'al* is able to sneak into a woman's house because he looks like a cat or is the "size of a cat" (RML, tale 127). Interestingly, Black-man himself suffers from an inability to distinguish things. In the following tale, for example, he mistakes a horse for a person and is told he must be blind. In this story, *h'ik'al* begs the saints for company.

THE SPOOK (*hʔikʼal*) AND THE SAINTS

Once there was a spook who asked for permission from one, asked for permission from another. He went to the church of the Blessed Martyr [St. Sebastian]. "Marty, give me one or two of your children as presents, for I long to take them off to my house. They'll be company for me. I'll be happy [having someone] to talk to," said the man who arrived. But it wasn't a real man; it was a spook.

"Ah I don't know. I don't know what my younger brother Larry [St. Lawrence] would think. Go talk to Larry. Who knows what Larry will tell you. If Larry tells you, 'Take them,' then what else could I say?" said Marty.

[The spook] went to talk to Larry. "Larry, won't you please give me one or two of your children, because you have many now. It isn't as if you hadn't any children, it seems. You have many children, it seems," said the spook. [That's what] he told Larry.

"Me, I'll never give away my children. I'll never give my children. I'm content with my children. They remember to bring me my flowers. They remember to bring me my candles, at dusk and at dawn. Even if it isn't every one of them, but when it occurs to them, when they remember to come, then I'm satisfied. I won't give my children. And you, what have you brought me? What is it? You, what will you give me? Step aside, nuisance! Please don't get me angry or I'll hit you," St. Lawrence replied.

Oh, [the spook] waited awhile. Then he went to talk to the Blessed Martyr. "Marty, favor me with one or two of your children, your offspring, because I want them for company. I want to talk to them," he said.

"Oh, but you are certainly telling a lie. It isn't because you'll befriend them. It isn't because you'll talk to them. You'll go stick them somewhere in the mountains, in the caves. It isn't because you know how to talk. But me, I'm satisfied that they sweep my house, tidy my house, that they come to look after my house. They always come to give me my flowers. They always come to give me my candles. They always come to give me my incense. I'm happy with my children. It's true not all of them do that. Not all of them come to give me things like that. But whoever it is, they each take turns. One day, one. Another day, another. Or another day, none. But I'm satisfied with my children. You, what do you bring me? You, what do you offer me? You are just pestering and pestering [me] at dusk and at dawn. What do you come bringing me? 'Oh,

Marty, give me one of your children. Oh, Marty, give me one of your
sons, give me one of your daughters. Even if it's a girl, that's good
enough for me,' you say, you tell [me]. But, as for me, I won't give away
my children. I've been sick of this right from the start. Go, go to Johnny's
[St. John's] house. Maybe it won't take long if you want to talk to him."

"Oh I don't remember where Johnny's house is."

"Well, go talk to my younger brother, Larry. See what he tells you.
Try him out. But as for me, I've said that I certainly won't give them
away. I won't give them away, because I'm happy with them," he said.

[The spook] went. He just chattered away. "Larry, give me one of
your children, because I want one, I need one. I want company, I want
[someone] to talk to. I'm happy [if I have someone] to talk to there
where I live," said the horrible spook at Larry's place.

"Oh, if you want one I'll give you one because I'm just sick and tired
of this. You keep pestering me so. Go, look! One's coming over there.
Go look at that one! Go meet that one on the trail there! He's coming
there on the path," he said. But it was a great big mule he went to em-
brace. It was a good kicking he got. He landed way over there face up.

I don't know if it was the back of his head that he struck. For a long
time he felt the pain, [staying] there in his house. The horrible spook
returned home. He was sick. His head had been aching. I don't know if
it was for one week or two, or how long it was until it got well. "You
did that, Larry, you did that to me. Was it a human being? It wasn't a
human being you gave me. It was a great big mule."

"It's because you can't see well, you're blind. You know you don't
know how to look. The person was coming and he had a good laugh
when you landed over there on your back," said Larry.

But you know, "If only you weren't so mean-hearted. Come on, I guess
I'll talk to Marty. [I'll see] if he gives me [one]. If Marty says to me,
'Take him,' then I'll certainly take him," he said.

[The spook] went. He arrived there at Marty's. "Marty, favor me with
one of your children, because I want company. I want [someone] to talk
to. I'm content if they fix my meal when I go someplace."

"Where in the world do *you* go?"

"Oh, I go to the churches, I go visiting at the houses. I go wherever
I can find bread to eat. Because I only eat bread. I don't eat tortillas," he
said.

"Where in the world is your bread? Where in the world do you get
money to pay for the bread? It's just stolen by you. Stupid loafer, step
aside," said the Blessed Martyr.

"That's why I'm asking you."

"Oh, go, go take one! I've been sick and tired of this from the start. Go take one! There's one coming on the Chamula trail," he said. [The spook] quickly went to look. As it turned out, he went and hugged a horrible hawthorn tree, too.

"But Marty, I've hurt myself badly. Thorns stuck in my mouth, thorns stuck in my face. You just tricked me. It certainly was a horrible hawthorn I hugged."

"It's because you can't see. There he is walking away. It's because you can't see. Go look! There he is," [Marty] told him again.

"I guess I'll go look," he said. So then he landed in the river, submerged [in the river], pushed off the bridge by the kick of a mule that was crossing over. He landed in the river, submerged in the river. God, at that time the river was full. He was carried off by the river as far as Pumlahan ʔUk'um or wherever it was the spook was able to get out. You see, he got out. He was tossed out by the flooding river.

Maybe he didn't drown, maybe nothing happened to him. So he came again to talk the same way. "You know, I fell in the river."

"Don't fall in the river. It's because you walk on the edge of the bridge. The mule pushed you off, but mules walk on one side, people on the upper side. You can't succeed the way you are. Don't keep coming and making me lose my temper. You haven't anything to say to me anymore. Go look for someone else to give you others. [See] if there is someone who will offer them to you, but me, I won't give away my children. My children please me. My children are sick and tired of being frightened. You scare them so often. One came to complain yesterday. You see, you nearly dragged her out of her house. You see, you scared her. You see, you caught her chickens. You see, you killed her chicks. You see, you drank a water gourd full of eggs. Now, they were useful to my children to pay for my candles, to pay for my flowers. What happened to the poor [people's] eggs? You broke all of them. You sucked all of them. Are you a weasel that you drink my children's things? That's why I won't give you anything. Step aside! Go! Go to Johnny's country! Try it! He has lots. He has lots of children. But me, mine can be counted. I just have a few little children. Take a look [and see] if Johnny will give them to you," he said.

He arrived in his land, Johnny's land. "But what can I think up? What can I do? Would it be a good idea if I bought a candle? Would he be pleased with a candle? Or should I buy him cane liquor maybe. If I tell him, 'Let's drink!' would he drink?" said the spook. "Oh, but if he doesn't drink [my liquor]? It's better if I buy a candle," he said. He planted his candle at the church door so that the saint would hear him out, so that the saint would come out. Maybe he thought he would come out to talk. He rang the bell. "Bong," said the bell at midnight.

Oh, the poor Chamulas were scared. The Chamulas went. They went, went to look at their church. "The robber has already entered the church. There's no time left. Our saints will die. Let's go look. Let's go take care of our church," they said. The Chamulas blew their horns. They assembled. They swarmed out. The horrible spook was scared. He fled too, because the Chamulas gathered like that.

"But can't I find even one church that will be kind to me. Look, Johnny didn't give me even one of his children. His children gathered together. Their guns were cracking, just to kill me. You see, I fled. I was scared. That's why I came," he told his spook friend. He went to tell him there at his cave.

"But you go! You have always gone out. Go do your best, now that your face has been seen already, it seems. Go talk to him, but talk to Johnny alone! 'Johnny, give me one of your children. You have too many. You can't be happy letting them eat fish, letting them eat june bug grubs, letting them eat maggots. That isn't what you should give them. Give me one. Me, I won't eat him, not me! I want him for company,' you tell him," the other one said.

The [first spook] arrived there. He went to tell him that. "Give me one."

"Go take her. That's it! I'm sick and tired of this now," [St. John] said.

But you know the woman that was given to him was a little old lady. But the little old lady wasn't good for anything. She couldn't even see. Quickly at vespers he went to catch the little old lady. The little old lady just fainted with fear when the horrible spook carried her off. "Where are you taking me, son? Where are you taking me, son? Where are you going to leave me, son?" she cried when she was carried off.

"Wait nanita, wait nanita, wait nanita," answered the horrible spook.

"Where are you going to leave me, son? But I know my house has been left far behind already. I know my house is far away. Where are you leaving me?" That's what the little old lady was screaming. The little old lady's heart was worn out, because she was so terribly old. She fainted with fear. He just arrived and threw her in the cave when he arrived. She slept. The little old lady slept. It was just "Darling, let's sleep together! Darling, eat!" the spook was trying to say to her.

God, the little old lady didn't move now. She was just speechless. When dawn came on the next day, the little old lady was dead.

That horrible spook went to give candles. "This is how you tricked me. The little old lady you gave me is dead already. The old woman you gave me. She isn't alive. I just arrived to lay her down in my house. She only said to me, 'Where are you going to leave me?' 'Wait, nanita, I'm going to take you home! Wait, nanita, I'm going to take you home!' I told her. I thought she was fine. The little old lady you gave me was already dead. I thought she was alive," said the horrible spook. He went to tell Johnny. The little old lady he was given was very, very old. The little old lady hadn't the strength to speak anymore. She died of fright.

You see how it was, what it was that happened long ago. The way the spooks asked and asked permission of the saints, it seems. It was just one little old lady that was given to appease him. Not many were given.

The last time he went to ask for one, he was given a boy. But the boy was riding a horse. [The spook] endured the horse's kicking. The boy fell. Then [the spook] grabbed him and carried him off. The horse was left standing there. That was surely the first time he won. He just went and stuck the boy in a cave.

You know another time at the place where clay is dug [for making pottery], an old Chamula lady was digging clay, it seems. She had a little girl. Her little girl was maybe twelve or fifteen years old or so. "Take your clay, daughter. Go take it home. Meanwhile, knead it after you arrive," she told the girl.

"All right," said the girl. She was kneading her little bit of clay by the door. But you see, her grandmother hadn't arrived when he came whooshing down. She thought it was a buzzard standing there. [The grandmother] arrived at her door. Then she saw that the poor girl had been taken off. [The spook] went. He carried her off. "Just stay there, girl, just stay there! We have returned home now. See which chicken you'll eat. [Do you want] to eat the black hen or [do you want] to eat the barred one? See which one! Kill it! Then put aside my share for me. I'll come back to eat. As for me, I'm going to bring food for us," said the horrible spook.

"All right," answered the girl. But she was upset, stuck in a deep cave. She cooked her meal. She had pots, bowls, gourds, whatever [she needed] to prepare her meal. She prepared it. She ate. But, you know [the spook] just ate meat, not tortillas, not the things you eat. He just had meat.

They ate. They ate the meat. The spook arrived. He had carried off a crate of bread. "Here is the bread for your meal. Cook your meal! Eat! You have nothing to worry about. Please don't be sad!" he said.

But, you see, on the third night after her arrival the girl had a child. A little baby spook was born. As for the baby spook, the woman took sick [because of him]. The woman told how her child was born, the little baby spook, it seems. "Nanita, nanita," that's how the baby spook talked. Who knows if it grew up in one night. Who knows how the spook grew up to talk that way. The girl was frightened by it. "Why does my child talk like this? Why does it say 'Nanita'? My Lord, but can it be some kind of dirty business? Could his father be a devil?" she said. For the poor girl didn't know what it was that had carried her off.

You see, when hunters passed by on the trail, "Hoo heigh come take me out. Look at me, because I'm helpless. I'm sick now. I don't want to to be here anymore. The cold is terrible. I'm suffering terribly from the cold where I am. I hadn't any [warm] clothes when I was brought here. Who are you?" she asked. "Is it you, uncle?"

"It's me, niece. What do you want, for I've come looking for you?" asked the gentleman. "What do you have to tell me, niece?"

"I came here. I'm sick. I have a child now. It's the child of the man I came with. Take me out, uncle.' "

"Wait, I'll get my lasso, I'll get it. I'll get you out on condition, niece, that your husband isn't there. He'll kill us. I'll get you out [on condition] that he doesn't shoot us," said the Chamulas.

"No uncle, he has gone to bring bread for us to eat. Don't be afraid uncle! Don't be afraid! Please take me away, uncle, because I'm already beginning to swell here in the frightful cold. I feel awful. I feel awful in this terrible cold, uncle. Please may the holy virgin enter thy beautiful heart, uncle. Take me away."

"Grab the lasso, tie it around your waist! Grab the end of it," he told her. He threw his lasso down [to her]. Three lengths of rope went into the cave. Oh, the woman came out with difficulty.

But you see, "Nanita, nanita," said the horrible spook coming up hanging on to her skirt. Her child [was clinging] to the hem of her skirt.

"Pull it off with your hand, niece! Throw it off! It's on the hem of your skirt. Don't you bring up the spawn of your companion in deviltry," said her uncle.

"All right, uncle," she said. With one hand she held on to the rope, with the other hand she grabbed it and threw it down. That "Nani—ta" could still be heard inside the cave from that horrible baby spook.

Then the woman came out. So then they took her away. They went to leave her at her house. They looked for the girl's house. They went to leave her at her house.

The poor girl had already begun to swell up. It was a sign of her having been submerged in water. Who knows how many days. She was submerged for a long time in water. Because it seems that her dirt had washed off. Her face was completely white. That's what the face of that poor girl was like. But she didn't last long. It was only three months and three weeks that she was alive. She died. She just reached home and died. For the girl's swelling had already begun. It was because the horrible spook's penis was so long. His penis was six feet long. That's why she told her uncle, "Come, take me out!" Because she knew she was dying. The swelling had already begun. She just reached home and died (RML, tale 130).

H?ik'al is a rapist, a kidnapper, and a murderer, yet, strangely, his intentions are not entirely clear. Unquestionably he is sinister, but he also seems sometimes pathetic. When he beseeches the patron saints of Zinacantan to give him one of their children, h?ik'al claims that what he desires is human companionship, "someone to talk to" (RML, tales 68 and 130). Nevertheless, these protestations mask a murderous, perhaps even cannibalistic, intent. When he does obtain someone, Black-man, supposedly without meaning to, frightens her to death.

That h?ik'al may be a cannibal is suggested by his promise to San Lorenzo when he is begging for a person to keep him company: "Johnny, give me one of your children. You have too many. You can't be happy letting them eat fish, letting them eat june bug grubs, letting them eat maggots. That isn't what you should give them. Give me one. Me, I won't eat him, not me! I want him for company" (RML, tale 130). In the tales where h?ik'al murders a woman, the first indication that she is dead is her blood boiling on the fire making the sound pululu. This cooking also suggests that h?ik'al consumes the blood of his victims.[6] Whether or not Black-

---

[6] It is interesting to note here the similarities between Black-man and the vam-

man is actually a vampire-type, the Zinacanteco narrator makes it clear that his is not a normal human diet: Black-man "just ate meat, not tortillas, not the things you eat." (RML, tale 130). Similarly, in Field Interview-8 the informant Domingo de la Torre Perez describes *hʔikʼal* as saying, "I only know how to eat bread;[7] I don't know how to eat tortillas." Besides attacking dogs and pigs, *hʔikʼal* is a notorious chicken thief, with a voracious appetite for raw eggs. In tale 130 he is accused of eating a water gourd full of stolen eggs. He is also known to pilfer beans (Field Interview-8). In other words, *hʔikʼal* seems to eat just about everything *except* tortillas— which would be the staple food of a Zinacanteco. The emphasis, however, seems to be on meat. When the mother of *hʔikʼal* decides to send him some food, it is dried-up meat (RML, tale 124).

One curiously unsolved mystery about *hʔikʼal* is his color. The name itself is almost certainly derived from the Tzotzil adjective *ʔikʼ*, meaning "black" or "dirty," but no explanation is ever offered as to why he should be this color. In both myth and ritual, however, his blackness is always assumed. Sometimes *hʔikʼal* is associated or even confused with other black creatures—buzzards, black cats, and perhaps bats.

In the Tzotzil world (as well as in other parts of the Maya area) black is the color associated with the dead. For example, the Indians of San Pedro Chenalhó choose black candles when they want to represent or communicate with dead persons (see Guiteras-Holmes 1961: 295 and glossary definition for *ʔikʼ kantela*). By extension, black may also be associated with rottenness and bad smell. In treating the spook tales as a single body of material, I noticed equivalences between black charcoal and dead bodies (both are food for spooks) and between corpses and rotten wood (spooks may turn into these substances). Although there is no definite evidence connecting the color black with rottenness, the noun form of *ʔikʼ* invites speculation. According to the Tzotzil dictionary compiled for the Harvard Chiapas files by Robert Laughlin, *ʔikʼ*

---

pires of Eastern Europe, flying black demons associated with blood, death, and eroticism.

[7] While tortillas are considered normal fare for Zinacantecos, bread is a food associated with ladinos, suggesting that *hʔikʼal,* like them, has foreign ways.

may also mean "wind" or "air," especially wind in the body or odor (also the kind of wind that carries sickness). The word *yan yik'* means unpleasant odor and often has sexual overtones.

It may be that *hʔik'al* was inspired by black slaves who are known to have escaped to the highlands shortly after the Conquest, or else by Negro road-builders who worked in Chiapas some years ago. Features like Black-man's kinky hair (RML, tale 123) would substantiate this idea. Calixta Guiteras-Holmes, who worked among the Tzotzil Maya of San Pedro Chenalhó, holds the view that *hʔik'al* there derives from soot-faced Maya priests of classic Maya times (1961:335). An even more likely prototype for *hʔik'al*, however, is the ancient Maya bat god, a black demon who was associated with eroticism, blood, and sacrifice.[8] The ancient Maya treatment of the bat symbol will be discussed in the next chapter.

It is important to remember that no symbol is static; all the above possibilities may be relevant. Suppose that *hʔik'al* is a carry-over from ancient times. A tale from Chamula provides us with one example of how historical events may have modified his image. In this area, *hʔik'al* is a *pucuj* (*pukuh*), or devil, who goes about at night catching men, women, and children. He carries them off to where large machines are being used for highway construction. His next action is strange for Black-man; he feeds his captives to the machine, in order that the machines will be powerful and continue to function (Arciniega 1947:473–474). Though this tale lends support to the idea that Black-man might have a connection with Negro road-builders, it does not preclude the possibility that *hʔik'al* already had a clearly defined personality; new traits were simply amalgamated with established attributes. In order to understand the logic behind this tale, we need to take into account ancient beliefs about sacrifice: only by "feeding" human hearts to the sun god could the cosmic order be maintained. Yet, it is unlikely that any ancient had a bulldozer in mind.

[8] The Yucatec word derived from *ʔik'*, *ʔik'el*, means insect, or winged insects in general. In chapter 4, the relation between *hʔik'al* and the bat is discussed; the bat is an animal classified by the Tzotzil Maya as a *pepenetik*, along with butterflies and flying squirrels. This is a tantalizing linguistic tidbit, but I can find no evidence from Zinacantan that relates the name *hʔik'al* with a class of "winged insects."

If the descriptions of Black-man are compared from town to town in Highland Chiapas, sinisterness is a striking constant. In Cancuc (a Tzeltal Maya town), San Pedro Chenalhó, and Chamula (both Tzotzil-speaking), he is a black *pucuj* (or demon) inimical to man (Arciniega 1947:473–474 and Guiteras-Holmes 1961: 248). In the Tzotzil community of Oxchuc, human ills are blamed on *hʔik'al*. He is considered responsible for certain people being retarded; victims he carries off are returned as idiots (Villa Rojas 1946:309–310). The *hʔik'aletik* of San Pedro Chenalhó live in caves; they are seen by people who go out late in the afternoon to catch rats (Guiteras-Holmes 1961:263). As in Zinacantan, the people there insist that it is due to *hʔik'aletik* that people must lock themselves in their houses from four or five in the afternoon on.

In San Pedro Chenalhó, the fox, the owl, and especially the jaguar are animals associated with night, darkness, and evil. Along with the *hʔik'aletik*, these animals are constantly doing battle with a hummingbird who is identified with good. Throughout his interview, the Pedrano informant dichotomizes the evil of the jaguar's team and the good of their hummingbird opponent, who bears the epithet "man's preserver." "All the *wayhels* [*vayihel* "animal souls"] tried also in the struggle against the *natik'ilhol* [*hnatikil-hol*],[9] the *'ik'al* [*hʔik'al*]. The humming bird [*sic*]—the *ts'unun* [*ƈ'unun*]—was the bravest of all, we say, because it was he who vanquished the enemies of man" (Guiteras-Holmes 1961:248).

In Chamula, this antagonism between good and evil is also given cosmic overtones. *Cholmetik* (*hƈ'ul-meʔtik*) the moon, and *chultotic* (*hƈ'ul-totik*) the sun are pitted against the *hʔik'aletik*. An eclipse means that the sun has been lost temporarily.[10] Should devils ever completely triumph and the sun be destroyed, all mankind would perish (Arciniega, 1947:474).

Thus, in Chamula and San Pedro Chenalhó, *hʔik'al* is intimately involved with cosmic issues, with forces like the sun and the moon,

---

[9] According to Guiteras-Holmes, *natik'ilhol* (*hnatikil-hol*) is a long-haired mythical being that is able to fly; it is compared to the Lacandon Indians (1961: glossary definition).

[10] In Zinacantan, the word *ʔik'ubel* ("eclipse") is a derivative of the word for "black."

and with creatures like the hummingbird and the jaguar—symbols
that received complicated attention in the religions of ancient
Mexico. This association raises the possibility of similar antiquity
for *hʔikʼal*.

> Eating a chicken feathers and all is pretty close
> to eating a person clothes and all, and the way
> we're heading, if the people in these parts keep on
> getting hungry, some day they're going to eat us
> all up! (Asturias 1967)[11]

2.. *Hʔikʼal* in Ritual

If *hʔikʼal* leads a vivid existence in the imaginations of Zinacantecos, he also has a lively incarnation in the
person of ceremonial clowns who bear the same name and who
share in his reputation for being lascivious. On two occasions during
the busy ceremonial year, Zinacanteco attention is called to the antics
of Black-men. At San Sebastian, a fiesta of year renewal and office
change, five of the outgoing *mayoletik*[12] blacken their faces and
arms with ashes and dress up in leather pants and jackets. A sixth
wears a blue mask with white rings about the mouth and eyes and
the clothes of a ladino woman. At the second fiesta, *karnaval*, young
Zinacantecos, who need not be cargoholders, volunteer to be
hʔikʼaletik. They wear ladino-style clothing, but do not blacken
their skin. Only their leader, the *tot hʔikʼal*, rubs soot on himself.
As at San Sebastian, one of their number is a woman; she is referred
to as the "wife" of *tot hʔikʼal*. The other Black-men are sometimes
called his children. Unlike the *mayoletik*, the same man may play
this role year after year. He wears an old black hat, a long-sleeved
collarless shirt, brown breeches, an old brown army coat, and, over
the army coat, a large blanket with brown and white patches.

San Sebastian takes place January 19–22. It lasts a day longer

---

[11] From *Mulata* (1967) by Miguel Asturias. Reprinted by permission of Delacorte Press. (A Seymour Lawrence book.)

[12] "Junior" members of a hierarchy of offices called "cargos" that different
Zinacanteco men hold each year; *mayoletik* are equivalent to our policemen or
constables. Each office-holder is expected to finance certain ceremonial events.
Usually the amount spent is representative of the prestige attached to the cargo.

than most other fiestas and involves extensive advance preparations. *Karnaval* fills the first five days preceding Lent. Descriptions of these fiestas can be found in the fieldnotes of Frank Cancian, Nick Colby, Robert Laughlin, and Manuel Zabala, and in the appendices of John Early's dissertation "The Sons of Saint Lawrence." In terms of this work, Victoria Reifler Bricker's notes and her doctoral thesis "The Meaning of Laughter in Zinacantan" offer many insights into the nature of *hʔik'aletik*; in particular she provides material on what the performers are actually saying to one another. The clearest accounts of the two rituals appear in Evon Z. Vogt's monograph *Zinacantan*, part 4. Much of the material presented here is taken from Vogt's account. By focusing particularly on the part played by *hʔik'aletik* in these ceremonies, I am being overselective perhaps. It is important to remember that a lot of other things are going on, both between the events described here and simultaneously with them.

At San Sebastian the whole group of outgoing officials to which the *hʔik'aletik* belong are called *htoy-k'inetik* ("entertainers"). Entertainment seems to be a key element in the impersonations at both fiestas. "When the alfereces change [at San Sebastian] those who joke the most are the outgoing alfereces" (VRB 106 072). *Karnaval* is called *k'in tahimoltik* ("Fiesta of Games"). The *tot hʔik'al* is chosen for his stamina and his reputation for sexuality, but also for his sense of humor—especially his ability to tell a dirty joke. The word used here for "game" is *tahimoltik* from the Tzotzil verb *tahin*, which means "play," "frolic," or "wrestle." This same word is used by *hʔik'al* in RML, tale 123. He accosts two travelers and asks them if they want to "play," or fight; what he seems to mean is a kind of contest (which makes me wonder about the ceremonial jousting at San Sebastian—how does this idea of play-fight fit in?). In addition, the word *tahintavan* means "to deceive a person repeatedly" (translations are from Laughlin's Tzotzil dictionary). In one of the conversations recorded by Victoria Bricker at San Sebastian, an officeholder asks the female *hʔik'al*, "Are you untrustworthy?" She replies: "No you're the one who is untrustworthy—I'll just carry you off." Of course, she *is* deceiving him; as a human dressed as *hʔik'al*, and as a man dressed up like a woman, deceit is implicit in her role. The accusation and her denial only emphasize the masquerade.

Some notion of game seems to be involved in the incidence of role reversal at these festivals—especially at San Sebastian. The impersonators have temporary license to ignore proprieties. The *hʔikʼaletik* run riot, ridiculing people and "capturing" visiting spectators (Chamula boys). They dance not just forward but also backward, because they are "loco" and forget how to dance correctly (Vogt 1960: Field Interview-2).[13] They pervert the norms of good conduct, threatening to eat or to castrate their prisoners if not given food. The characterization of their role seems to oscillate between irony and appropriateness. Constables associated with order impersonate the Black-men notorious for kidnap, thievery, and unrestrained sexuality. Conversations between these characters and their audience indicate that *hʔikʼaletik* are also adulterous and incestuous. In social terms, it is hard to imagine a figure more disorderly! At the same time, as we shall see, these constables are supposed to publicly denounce absent officials for negligence and for *their* preoccupation with sexuality.

In addition to these overtones of play and irony, the characterizations at San Sebastian abound with role reversals like that of the sixth *hʔikʼal*. This man impersonates an animallike black demon who is dressed as a very civilized, white, ladino woman. While the other *hʔikʼaletik* carry stuffed animals, she holds a white baby doll. Real oppositions appear to be dramatized here: between nature and culture, civilized and uncivilized, man and animal. Another set of characters suggests even more strongly that these kinds of oppositions are at work. The *hkašlan* and *hšinulan*[14] are costumed as Colonial Spanish gentlemen and Spanish ladies. Rosaries and mirrors hang from their necks and wrists. The *sak-holetik* ("white

---

[13] Interestingly, another spook, the *xtabai* (Yucatán and Belize), which walks backwards, is likewise connected with these dual themes of role reversal (she is a demon behaving like a human) and deceit (she impersonates her victim's sweetheart). The reason given for her habit is that she is keeping her hollow back from view. In Zinacantan there is a spook known as *hvalopatʔok* whose feet walk forwards and backwards (personal communication from Robert Laughlin).

[14] Terms designating men and women ladinos.

heads") are dressed in white with red turbans. They too wear rosaries and mirrors. Each carries a bow, an arrow, and a rattle. These
three types belong to the group of "senior" entertainers. The *hʔik'-
aletik*, the *bolometik* (men costumned as jaguars), the *k'uk'ul čon*
(the name means literally "plumed serpent," but they are costumed
as ravens), and the *ton-teʔetik* (Spanish-moss wearers referred to
as Lacandones) [15] are all "junior" entertainers.

The two groups of senior and junior entertainers appear to be
divided into civilized and uncivilized; there is a contrast between
civilized men who wear ladino clothes and carry "culture" symbols
(rosaries, mirrors, weapons, music-makers), and uncivilized, spotted, or feathered animals, moss-covered jungle savages, and black
demons. Implicit in these oppositions between civilized and uncivilized, man and animal, white and black is the contrast between pro-
priety and impropriety, proper sex and promiscuity.

In Zinacantan, men are distinguished from animals by having
"reason"; that is, they have knowledge of and respect for the proper
way of behaving at rituals and in relations with other people. Especially significant in distinguishing men from animals is the capacity
men have for speech. Unlike animals, men have learned certain
spoken formulas for attaining what they want. Whoever does not
respect these human norms in behavior will be called an animal
(Bricker 1968:163).

In accord with Zinacanteco criteria, the *hʔik'aletik* at this fiesta
comport themselves like animals. Several of the characters played
by junior entertainers have animal sounds peculiar to them: the
two *k'uk'ul čon* make a "hur, hur" noise; the *bolometik* go "huh,
huh, huha." the characteristic sound of *hʔik'aletik* is "veš, veš,
veš."[16] When the *hʔik'al* does speak, it is to say something insulting
or blasphemous. Toward the end of one of many visits made during San Sebastian to the houses of cargoholders, the father of an

----

[15] Lacandones are a Maya people living in the jungles of lowland Chiapas. Even
the rudiments of Western technology (that Zinacantecos have picked up) have
not yet touched them. In myth, it was these "savages" who agreed to murder San
Sebastian when no one else would.

[16] This sound, made with the hands, is that of the *turukuk* (an owl) (Vogt
1960: Field Interview-2).

official says to *hʔik'al*, "You don't have grace because you fuck your co-mother."[17] The Black-man mocks serious conventions when he replies "What does it matter . . . as long as a son is born" (Bricker 1968:275). Unquestionably, *hʔik'al* is encouraged to act this way; there is a great deal of spectator understanding of, and complicity in, his performance. The *hʔik'al* says: "Comadre don't tell my compadre about any of this! Let us fuck each other at once . . ." His compadre, another Black-man, answers: "I won't be angry. Do it, for the woman desires it very much, ha, ha, ha. You can look at the child when it's born to see if it has my face . . ." (Bricker 1968:275).

The *hʔik'aletik* are adulterous and, by Zinacanteco standards, incestuous. Behaving like their mythic counterparts, these Black-men seize young Chamula bystanders and threaten to eat or to castrate them. That they are indeed cannibals is suggested again when they trade their captives for some food. Although they are clearly not real animals (they talk and have ritual kin among Zinacantecos), their fantastic conduct makes it impossible to consider them human either.

These oppositions between human and animal, civilized and uncivilized, are themselves ambiguous. The masquerading *hkašlam* would appear to epitomize what is civilized, but, as a foreigner, he also represents what is distant and non-Zinacanteco. Thus, there is a correspondence between a foreigner and an animal, or a creature (like *hʔik'al*) who behaves like an animal. In Tzotzil usage, the words *hkašlan* and *kašlan* ("chicken") both derive from *castellano*. The obvious explanation is that both the Spaniards and the chickens they brought with them are foreign or imported, but this correspondence may have deeper implications: though the ladinos seem "cultured" and perhaps even more "sophisticated" than Zinacantecos, they are also ignorant of Zinacanteco norms and, as such, are socially distant, as are animals.[18] Another figure, the *ton-teʔ*, represents a Lacandon, also a foreigner, who seems to have the status of an animal (also jungle-living) like the jaguar.

---

[17] Zinacantecos regard sexual relations between ritual kin as incestuous.

[18] I cannot deal with the full complexity of this contradiction, but it involves one of the most painful aspects of social change, when an intact culture is forced to deal with a technologically superior culture.

The *k'uk'ul čon* is likewise ambiguous. He wears a white shirt with green and red dots and a white hat with red dots.[19] Attached to the hat is a beak holding an ear of corn. He wears small wings strapped to his back. He clearly represents an animal, the raven, which, however, is no ordinary bird. He is a scavenger who comes to men's fields and eats men's food. In the Maya creation myths, it is the raven that stole corn from the earth and gave it to man in the first place. As such, in the vocabulary of Lévi-Strauss, he is doubly a mediator between nature and culture.

The association of *h'ik'aletik* with animals and also with foreigners is repeatedly emphasized. Clearly they are malefactors who belong to an order separate from Zinacantecos. For instance, this distinction emerges in how and what the *h'ik'aletik* eat. The Black-men at San Sebastian, like their counterparts in myth, are cannibals who threaten to eat their Chamula captives. The *tot h'ik'al* at *karnaval* eats at a separate table of his own and is given double portions.[20] Although there is no mention of cannibalism it may be that he eats raw meat; the chicken that he is given to take home in his net bag is only half-baked and still partially feathered (Zabala Fieldnotes 1957–1960:59). Traditionally at *karnaval*, there are only two people who serve *chicha*, a special ceremonial drink: the *tot h'ik'al* and a Chamula hired for the occasion. A comparison of events between the two fiestas might likewise suggest a connection between *h'ik'al* and foreigners, or at least between *h'ik'al* and someone who is not a Zinacanteco. At San Sebastian, the *h'ik'aletik* chase and capture Chamulas, whereas at *karnaval* it is the *tot h'ik'al* and his henchmen who are captured.

The time of San Sebastian is itself one of ambiguity; it is a period of role change and year renewal. San Sebastian is the first opportunity for new officials to celebrate a major fiesta. Nevertheless, although they help in the way of supplies and arrangements, theirs is a spectator's role—they learn perhaps how not to behave in office. The real protagonists are the outgoing officials—some of whom left

[19] It may be that spots, like the color black, are considered more like "nature." The jaguar also has spots; the *ton-te'etik* are covered with moss.

[20] These large portions may also reflect an analogy between appetite for food and sexual incontinence.

office as long ago as the preceding August. It is an appropriate time for housecleaning, for bringing past misconduct into the open, and for admonishing new recruits to behave well. It is a time to define roles, but also a time of role ambiguity. Participation involves men who are both in and out of office; much public attention is centered on men who were in office but who behaved as though they were not.

Among the odd details of this fiesta are the names given to each of the four days:

> "day of jousting" (*čan-k'obol*)
> "day of first banquet" (*ba veʔel*)
> "day of no banquet" (*muʔyuk veʔel*)
> "day of last banquet" (*slaheb k'ak'al veʔel*)

One of the distinguishing features of being in office is participation in ritual meals. It could be that an analogy of the following order is at work here:

> *being in office*: *not being in office*::
> *meal*: *no meal*
> or, *coming into office*: *leaving office*::
> *first meal*: *last meal*

Though the situation is wrought with ambiguity, certain definitions are being fashioned, which have to do with the requirements of a certain role and what kind of people fail to fill the role.

This concern with offices not properly fulfilled is articulated throughout the fiesta of San Sebastian. On three consecutive nights of the fiesta (January 16, 17, and 18), the previous year's hierarchy visits the church of San Sebastion to ask forgiveness for misconduct during their term of office. On January 22, the junior entertainers, dressed as *hʔik'aletik*, light candles and pray for any poor performance during their past year's cargo. The high point of the entertainment is the ridicule of defaulting cargoholders who have failed to show up for this last exercise of office. Supposedly, they have been more interested in sex than in their official responsibilities. It is the business of the *hʔik'aletik* to publicly denounce these cargoholders. In particular, their jibes are aimed at the men who failed to show up for this final exercise, but their ridicule may apply to anyone whose performance in office has been inadequate. By extension, the wives of these cargoholders are also implicated.

In addition to the six policemen impersonating *h'ik'aletik*, there are two other outgoing officials who are dressed in costumes of orange brown material with black circles and white dots painted on. Their tails and hats are real jaguar fur. These are the *bolometik*, or jaguars, mentioned above. Both the *bolometik* and *h'ik'aletik* carry stuffed animals and pointed sticks which they use as props in ridiculing the defaulting cargoholders. The *h'ik'aletik* carry stuffed squirrels, iguanas, and spider monkeys, while the *bolometik* carry squirrels, iguanas and coatis. These stuffed animals represent the wives of the cargoholders. They are painted red on their undersides to emphasize their genitals. About the animals' necks hang the necklaces and ribbons that their husbands supposedly bought with funds earmarked for cargo expenses. When the *h'ik'aletik* poke at the squirrels' genitals with pointed sticks, also painted red at the tips, the symbolism is made doubly explicit by the comments of the performers: "Look at Marian Peres from Masan [a constable who did not finish his term of office]. He's nothing but a fucker. That's what he does all the time at the foot of a Mango tree" (Bricker 1968:271–273).[21]

Supposedly, Marian Peres has been at home with his wife instead of performing his cargo duty; this behavior is doubly blasphemous since cargoholders are forbidden to have intercourse during fiestas. Similarly, another defaulting cargoholder, Lol ʔUč is accused of unrestrained sexuality and of having intercouse at improper times in inappropriate places. The Black-man speaks to a group of women in the same house with him: "Look, my mother, look my lady at what Lol ʔUč is doing with Maruč [is wife]. How shameless they are, always fucking each other, even when not in their own home!" Then he says to the squirrel: "Now don't *you* kneel and fuck here. Is this your house here? Yes you may join the musicians but don't fuck each other by the fire!" (Bricker 1968:271) People accused of being promiscuous or of having intercourse all the time or in improper places are considered animals. Marian and Loša are de-

---

[21] The names listed here and elsewhere have, of course, been changed.

scribed as copulating, "like animals in a pigpen" (Bricker 1968: 162).

Apparently, Lol ʔUč has not only been negligent, but he has also behaved intemperately while in office. In spite of the heavy drinking required of them in office, cargoholders are not supposed to get drunk. Yet, Lol ʔUč is accused of just that. The jaguar performer tells Lol that he is going to have to extract the soul[22] of Lol's little son from the ground to where it fled when his father became drunk in office.

The defaulting cargoholder does not bear the burden of his sins alone. The sticks and also the tails of the squirrels are used to represent his penis, but, as mentioned, the squirrels themselves are the *wives* of cargoholders. These squirrels are said to be women who have no shame. On their visits to the homes of cargo officials, the *hʔik'aletik* lay the squirrels next to the fire. They tell the women who are there grinding corn that *they* are different from these animals, because they have shame and do not perform sexual intercourse in public (Bricker 1968:257). A man who has succumbed to sexual temptation at a time when he should have abstained is considered weak. His wife on the other hand is considered too strong for a woman; she is over-sexed. This is what is meant by the jibe, "Maruč [the woman] is above and Lol ʔUč is below!" (Bricker 1968:272). This insult refers to a role reversal between husband and wife; it also provides the proper contrast between a woman who is too "strong" and the man who has been too weak.

At *karnaval*, none of these accusations are directed against cargoholders. Rather, it is the *hʔik'aletik* themselves who are being dealt with. On Tuesday, two ceremonial banquets take place, one at the house of the Junior Pasionero, where the *karnaval* performers eat, the other at the Hermitage, where the civil officials and (following them at a second sitting) the Alfereces are fed.[23] At these banquets,

---

[22] In traditional Maya beliefs still partly shared by many Zinacantecos, souls are divided into thirteen parts, any one of which may be lost due to a great fright or other causes.

[23] The position of Alferez is an important one, second highest in the hierarchy; the position of the Pasioneros is less important. The Hermitage of Esquipulas is where officials are sworn into office.

the *tot hʔik'al* and his *hʔik'aletik* carry messages between the two groups. These contain jokes and charges against the *hʔik'al*. In the events that follow, the demons and their leader are repeatedly chased and captured. Time after time their cooperative captors allow them to escape—which leads to another wild run through the audience. Finally, the *tot hʔik'al*, who is the last to be imprisoned, is safely in jail along with his henchmen, their wrists bound. The *karnaval* officials come to plead with the Presidente for their release —which is granted.

It may be that the *hʔik'aletik* at *karnaval* are more generalized figures representing mischief-makers. These *hʔik'aletik* are called *pukuh*, a term for demons. There does not seem to be the same emphasis on either neglected office or improper sex that there is at San Sebastian—though it may be that the issue of sexuality is implicit in the identity of *hʔik'al*. Before discussing these differences, I would like to point out an interesting similarity, although it is hard to know how much significance to accord it. Both the *hʔik'aletik* of San Sebastian and the demons of *karnaval* are involved with some aspect of food exchange. At San Sebastian they bargain with the officials for food in exchange for the Chamula boys they have captured. They take this food to the *Bolom Teʔ* (Jaguar Tree), climb up, and throw the food down to their fellows.[24] The stuffed animals are also fed bits of food. These are tossed back and forth between the *hʔik'aletik* in the trees and those on the ground.

Likewise, at *karnaval*, the *tot hʔik'al* makes a special "chocolate" —a concoction of brown sugar, finely ground coffee, and rum— which he gives to the banqueting officials. In return, they give him food. He also gives to each member of the Ayuntamiento and to two Mayordomos a lime and a small bunch of onions. In exchange, he receives food, eggs, and tortillas.[25]

---

[24] This business of throwing food down from trees is an old pattern in Maya myth and ritual, occurring in the *Popol Vuh* and cited for Yucatec and Guatemalan ceremonies.

[25] It is interesting to note that the impersonating *hʔik'aletik* do not hestiate to eat tortillas, while *hʔik'aletik* in myth explicitly do not. They eat only bread (ladino food) and meat.

Although the behavior of *tot hʔik'al* of *karnaval* cannot be connected explicitly with deviation from norms and punishment for neglecting duty, recurring patterns of events at the Christmas festival in Zinacantan as well as parallels in fiestas involving Black-men in other Maya towns suggest that the two may be connected. At the ceremonies held for the Virgen de Pascua (December 15–25), there are no Black-men. Instead, two groups of characters called *mamaletik* and their wives, *meʔ-čunetik*, are the malefactors. They are codefendants at a mock trial; supposedly they cannot produce papers to show that they really own the "torito."[26] This trial is perhaps comparable to the exchange of damning notes that goes on during the banquets at *karnaval*. At any rate, the Presidente gives orders for the Mayores to put the *mamaletik* in jail. As at *karnaval*, there is a prolonged chase (their pursuers even release them several times in order to make it last) until they are finally caught and jailed. At *karnaval, tot hʔik'al* is released because of the intervention of the officials; at the other festival the wives of the *mamaletik*[27] come to plead their husbands' case. After about fifteen minutes' imprisonment, they are let go.

One important theme that comes up in this Christmas–New Year's festival is the chastisement of women who have not performed appropriately their role as women. Part of the job of the *meʔ-čunetik* is to give the women a "sewing lesson" and to publicly single out those women who are not good weavers. Since making her husband's clothes is an important attribute of a good wife, this mockery is painful criticism. The *mamaletik* also have a hand in admonishing women to behave in a proper manner. They tell them: "Wash the lime-soaked kernels well[28] and take them to the mill! The girls must be accompanied by older women so that no boy will accost them on the path. Watch that the miller doesn't seize their hands! Count your change well . . . When the corn is ground, return together. When you get home make a lot of tortillas" (Bricker 1968:247).

----

[26] A symbolic bull killed during the fiesta.

[27] It may be significant that the brown deerskin breeches worn by *hʔik'aletik* are the same ones worn by the *mamaletik* (Vogt 1960: Field Interview-2).

[28] The same lime-water solution referred to in the myths.

Though it has only women as its object, the task of the *me²-čune-tik* closely parallels that of *h²ik'aletik* at San Sebastian who ridicule defaulting cargoholders and their wives. Both Bricker and Laughlin have pointed out how much San Sebastian in Zinacantan is like *karnaval* in other municipios. Their theory is that events originally part of *karnaval* have been moved up.[29] If such a time shift has occurred, the patterns would be complete at both fiestas, Christmas and the combined San Sebastian–*karnaval*: (1) remonstrators humiliate those who have not fulfilled their proper roles (as wives or as cargoholders); (2) these remonstrators who are themselves unruly are brought to trial, chased, jailed, and released.

Christmas	*San Sebastian*
Me²čunetik mock women who make poor wives	*H²ik'aletik* mock men who are weak and who give in to temptation, as well as wives who are too demanding

Karnaval

Me²čunetik and *mama-letik* are brought to trial; *mamaletik* are chased, jailed, and released	*H²ik'aletik* are condemned in letters, chased, jailed, and released

In her book about San Pedro Chenalhó, Guiteras-Holmes makes it clear that *h²ik'aletik* are associated with punishment. She defines *h²ik'aletik* as "the men with sooted faces who enact in carnival the role of legendary chastisers of sexual sin" (Guiteras-Holmes 1961: glossary).

Ritual buffoons who carry stuffed animals, which they poke with sticks, are apparently a widespread phenomenon in the Maya area. Sol Tax reports that black-clad ritual buffoons called "negritos" who have some kind of privileged license and who go about mimicking are found in many towns in Highland Guatemala. In Panajachel, the feast of Corpus Christi is the occasion of the "dance of negritos."

---

[29] Perhaps this jostling of events had to do with traditional difficulties between Indians who had one set of religious practices and Christian missionaries who sought their conformity to another set.

At San Pedro la Laguna[30] stuffed armadillos are used in the Cofradia[31] houses (quoted in Redfield 1936:239). Among the Yucatecan Maya of Quintana Roo[32] a man chosen for his ability to make people laugh is given the role of *chic*. To the Yucatec Maya this word means "laugh," as well as "coati" and "buffoon" (Redfield 1936:231–232, 239). Apparently, at some point in Maya tradition, buffoons were somehow identified with the small, anomalous (see chapter 4) animals that they carried.[33] Reminiscent of the people-snatching and sexual "offenses" of the *hʔikʔaletik* (they chase young Chamula bystanders and threaten to eat or to castrate them), the *chics*[34] of Dzitas, Yucatán, if they caught a small boy, removed his clothes and rubbed gunpowder in his anus. In the Yucatec barrio of "Santiago," the *chics* amuse crowds by lassoing men and fining them (Redfield 1936:241). Closely related to these Yucatec Maya are the Socotz Maya of Belize[35] (Redfield 1936:231). A connection exists there between ritual buffoons and stuffed animals. These clowns have special license in their behavior; they go about mimicking, and, indirectly at least, their behavior seems to involve dereliction of duty.

Among the Socotz the *chic* sits in the forest on top of a ceiba (silk-cotton) tree chopped down for the occasion. Around his shoulders he has a net bag with tortillas and a doll in it.[36] The tree is carried back to camp with the *chic* aloft, and the rest of the evening is spent dancing at the tree. In order to participate, each man pays a fee. Anyone who tries to dance without paying is led away

[30] Panajachel and San Pedro la Laguna are Quiché Maya towns around the shore of Lake Atitlán, Guatemala.

[31] Cofradia houses are the houses of religious groups in charge of the fiestas.

[32] Quintana Roo is a more remote, forested section on the Yucatec coast.

[33] A coati is a semi-arboreal raccoonlike animal with a long tail and a long nose with upturned proboscis. It lives in the forests of most of Central America and feeds on fruits, mollusks, small vertebrates, and turtle eggs (Stanek 1962: 498).

[34] There are two *chics*: one wears old clothes, a woven bag, and a feathered head-dress; the other is dressed, also in tatters, as a woman.

[35] Formerly British Honduras.

[36] All of these *chics* seem to carry a bag. The *tot hʔikʔal* also carries a basket with food. It might be helpful to know more about this doll and also the relation that might have existed in Zinacantan between the *tʔen tʔen* drum and the prototypical ceiba.

and tied to the ceiba tree (called *yaxche*) until he is ransomed (Thompson 1930:111–112). In these animal-buffoon dramatizations, there is the same interplay as at San Sebastian between men who are impersonating an animal-type being and men who are punishers of men who misbehave (or behave like animals?). These punishers are also punished (caught and jailed). The particular punishment dealt to *ħʔik'aletik* will be discussed later; are they really being punished or are they somehow being "tamed" and "rehabilitated"? As at *karnaval*, there are themes of capture and ransom connected with these buffoons. In the case of the Socotz at least, the capture is precipitated by failure to pay up—to do the thing a dancer at this ceremony should do.

As a final note to this section on San Sebastian and *karnaval*, I should mention something about the history of these fiestas. Elsewhere in Middle America, ceremonies featuring black men are derived from the mock battles between Christians and Moors that were first performed in medieval Spain and later adapted to the Conquest situation in the New World. Almost certainly, the Tzotzil Blackmen were once connected with these Moors. While I was revising this chapter, I received a letter from Robert Laughlin containing fascinating linguistic support for this view. He says that in Tzeltal, sorghum is called *moro ʔišim* "moorish corn," whereas in Tzotzil it is called *tukum ħʔik'al* "spook's corn." (No native plant is now known as *tukum*.) Furthermore, there are two adjectives, *moro* and *muruč'*, that mean curly leaved and that refer to a variety of cabbage and to diseased plants. It is unusual to have loan words with glottalized consonants, and these are presumed to be very early loans. It may be significant that "kinkiness" is one of these borrowed words, because curly hair is a trait commonly attributed to *ħʔik'al*.

It is unnecessary to assume that Tzotzil beliefs concerning Blackmen *originated* with a Catholic ceremony; rather, the Maya of Chiapas could have incorporated images selectively from the things that the Spanish exposed them to. In the first part of this chapter, a similar kind of adaptation was described whereby ancient beliefs about sacrifice were extended to include a bulldozer. Laughlin provides another example of this phenomenon; he suggests (1963:40) that the Maya throughout the Chiapas Highlands were especially attracted to San Sebastian—a Catholic martyr "bristling with arrows" —because of ancient customs whereby a sacrificial victim was transfixed with arrows. Perhaps Spanish black men, or "Moors," were singled out as items of special interest because they resembled a black creature already widely feared by the Maya. This creature may have been a bat demon, as will be discussed in chapter 3. Further evidence for the antiquity of *h?ik'aletik* are the props used and the other characters involved in these fiestas.

A prominent prop at San Sebastian is the *t'ent'en*, a special split drum kept by its owner in the hamlet of ?Elan Vo?. This drum, termed *teponaxtli* by the Aztecs, represented the "hollow tree," or ceiba, the divine tree of the Yucatec Maya, which was looked upon as a rain symbol. Since sacrifice by arrows (where blood spurts out on to the ground) would have been for them a symbolic plea for rain, it would have been logical to make the connection between drum and transfixed victim (Laughlin 1963:40).

In addition, the company kept by the *h?ik'aletik* at San Sebastian is too controversial to ignore. Although he is represented as a raven, *k'uk'ul ton* is an ancient name for "plumed serpent"—the deity who decorates the temples of Teotihuacan and Chichen Itza. The legends from San Pedro Chenalhó (Guiteras-Holmes 1961:263) describe the jaguar and the *h?ik'aletik* as forces of evil opposed to the hummingbird, man's savior. The placement of characters (like Hummingbird and Jaguar) prominent in the old religions of Middle America in such a "cosmic" context suggests a carry-over from ancient times. Interestingly, at San Sebastian there is a close association between Black-man and Jaguar, perhaps indicating that they belong to the same package of symbols. On the night before the main events of San Sebastian, Vogt reports (1960 notes) that the only characters wearing costumes were the *bolometik* (jaguars) and *h?ik'aletik*. One fieldworker describes these same Black-men trying, for some reason, to shake the jaguars out of the *Bolom Te?*, the "jaguar tree," they both had climbed (Early 1965:23).

In line with these speculations about the antiquity of *h?ik'al*, it is important to keep in mind the alternative view—that "these sym-

bols retain none of their original meaning" (Early 1965:26). My position in this paper differs from that view; I think that present messages concerning *hʔik'al*, as they are conveyed in myth and ritual, continue to reflect some connotations belonging to the ancient prototype. In the next chapter I hope to provide suggestions about what that prototype was like.

iii. The Ancient Maya Bat Symbol

Once, a bat fell to the ground and was caught by a weasel. When the bat pleaded for her life the weasel announced she was the enemy of all winged creatures. At that, the bat confessed that she was no bird, but a mouse, and was released. On another occasion, with the bat in a similar predicament, the weasel announced that she was the enemy of all mice. This time, the captive replied she was no mouse but a bat, and was again released (Aesop, c. 620 B.C.).

A black, winged, super-sexed demon also figured in ancient Maya mythology. He was the bat deity known in Nahuatl as *Tlacatzinacantli*—the source of the name Zinacantan. This bat was associated with blood and death and with other sacrificing creatures, the buzzard and the hummingbird.

1. The Sources and the Validity
of the Historical Approach

In suggesting what some of the associations of the ancient bat demon may have been, I will be drawing on sources covering a wide chronological and geographical span. The most ancient material comes from glyphs and stone carvings. Historic data are provided by the codices and the literature recorded by Maya speakers in Spanish script and by Spanish chroniclers. Current beliefs concerning the bat are available from ethnography. There is also the almost timeless source of the bat itself; presumably, the Maya noticed many of the same things about it in ancient times as we do today. Obviously, not all the connotations of the bat deity that will be covered here have occurred in the mind of any one individual at any one time. While some known associations may have been purely parochial, other unknown ones may have been widespread. Nevertheless, a composite of scattered connotations is perhaps as good a reconstruction as possible.

The greatest problem confronting this effort of reconstruction is to know how much of an analogy we can draw between ancient connotations and the present meaning attached to these symbols. Professional opinions differ concerning the relevance of archaeology and ancient literature to the current ethnographic scene. Some, like Eric Thompson, treat ancient beliefs and practices—even those among the Aztecs—as though they were highly relevant. In an article on contemporary Maya symbolism Thompson writes: "By delving into Aztec lore we have not only proved our connection between [three symbols] but we have shown once more the close association between Mayan and Mexican beliefs" (Thompson 1932:122). Another Mayanist, Rafael Girard, produced many volumes (*Los Chortis ante la Problema Maya*) based on a model that makes current Maya ethnography continuous with archaeological evidence. Needless to say, other Mayanists insist on a great deal more specificity, and they might well balk at the kinds of analogies that I will be making between the *hʔikʼal* as he appears today and the bat demon as he appears in ancient literature. But somewhere between over-enthusiasm and stalemate there may be a legitimate way to use this material. Though similarities between the ancient bat symbol and the *hʔikʼal* may also be influenced by structural factors, the situation is complicated by the genetic relation that exists between the ancient Maya and contemporary Tzotzil (Vogt 1964). At the end of this chapter I attempt a paradigm of some of the bat's connotations in ancient time. My suggestion is to use this very broad scheme as though it were relevant to contemporary material, as though the Maya area from classic to late classic times were homogeneous enough to allow for extrapolation from one site to another, and as though some current Maya beliefs derive from this base—but to do so with certain stipulations.

Symbols are complex and their meanings may shift from context to context. Different symbols may share connotations and become linked in this way, or the attributes of one symbol may become mixed with the attributes of another symbol. In a historical approach, there are additional complications to keep in mind.

1. More and more qualifications must crop up with increasing geographical and chronological distance from Zinacantan.

2. The ancient bat and *hʔikʼal* will coincide exactly in some attributes. Although a historical explanation is possible, the parallels could easily be the result of structural influences. It should be remembered that structural factors may also operate through time. (In this case it is questionable if a distinction can be made or if it is worthwhile to make the distinction.)

3. Some ancient attributes may be relevant only as they have indirectly affected the *aura* of the symbol. Because of the nature of symbols, it may be impossible to detach any one attribute from a cluster of meanings. (For instance, in Yucatán the bat symbol is connected with clouds, rain, and storms. Though these same connotations may not occur elsewhere, an association with darkness could be important.)

4. Even when a contemporary belief evolved from an older one, the ancestor belief may differ from the current version. In this case, certain central, or core, connotations (in the case of the bat and *hʔikʼal*, blood and black) are going to deserve more emphasis. This same principle applies to structural factors operating through time, where there may be a warping of emphases.

2. The Bat-Demon in Mesoamerica

The bat deity was widespread in Middle America. The bat, *piquite zina*, a name meaning "mouse skin," was the predominant figure on many Zapotec funeral urns. *Tzinacantli*—bat demon and "tearer off of heads"—appears in the Mexican Codex Borgia. Throughout the Maya area, the word used for bat, *zotz* (*soƶ'*), is constant.[1] Seler (1909) points out that the term *zotz* resembles the Mayan word *tzots* (*tzutz* in the Choloid group; spelled *ƶoƶ* in Laughlin's Tzotzil dictionary) meaning "hair" or "fur"; as with the Zapotec example, this association might underscore the anomalous character of the bat as a mammal with fur that also flies. However, Thompson later (1966) treats the two words as quite distant. At Copan, the bat was the site emblem, and two different groups of people called themselves *Zotzils* ("people of the bat"). A branch (clan?) of Cakchiquels worshipped the god *Zotzilha Chimalcan* ("controller of fire"), and took the bat as their symbol. In Chiapas, a tribe known as *Tzotzil uinic* settled, and the Nahuatl name Zinacantlan, "place of the bat," was given to their home by the Mexicans, who supposedly were referring to a great stone bat that was worshipped there. Ximenes mentions such a bat-stone, and the place is today the municipio of Zinacantan.

The most consistent attributes of the bat have to do with blood and sacrifice. Thompson (1966) points to the nature of the vampire bats in explaining the kind of logic that Mayans might have been using here. He reports that during the Colonial era attacks of vampire bats were given as the reason for abandoning at least two towns in Chiapas. He further suggests that the slow coagulation of blood from vampire wounds would have made the flow more copious, intensifying the association. The sacrifice glyph is frequently in-

fixed within the bat glyph,[2] as at Yaxchilan or Xculoc, or, as at Chichen Itza, the bat and sacrifice glyph may be subject to the same affix. According to Thompson, the death glyph is also associated

---

[1] Though the spellings *zotz* and *tsots* are frequently encountered, *soƶ'* is the spelling favored by Laughlin.

[2] Even though the Maya undoubtedly recognized different bat species, the deity as he is portrayed is a blend of outstanding traits. For instance, the prominent leaf-nose of *Phylostomidae* and the characteristic teeth of the vampire *Desmodus* are included in the same portrait head (see Thompson 1966).

with the bat; this glyph depicts an abstract heart with eyelashes
inscribed inside.

In the Mexican Codex Féjerváry-Mayer, *Tlacatzincantli* holds a
severed head in one hand, a heart in the other. In the Codex Vati-

canus, *arrancador de cabezas* holds two bleeding heads, and, like the
demon in Codex Borgia, has a nose that suggests a knife.

The bat is also linked with another sacrificing creature, the
vulture. The vulture and bat glyphs are frequently juxtaposed in ex-

amples from the Dresden Codex. One of the characteristic traits of
the vulture is to pluck out human eyes. This motif also appears on
the wing membrane of the Féjerváry-Mayer *Tlacatzinacantli*, as well
as on the cloak wings of a bat demon on a vase from Chamá, Guatemala (see illustration on page 66), illustrating how these two sacrifice personalities, bat and vulture, share the same attribute of goug-
ing out eyes.

Along with sacrifice, the bat-demon is linked with darkness and
the underworld. To reach the interior of the earth, the two heroes of
the Quiché Maya text, the *Popol Vuh*, must traverse the House of
Cold, the House of Jaguars, the House of Fire, the House of Knives,
and *zotzilha*, the House of Bats. In the House of Bats lives Camazotz,
the Death-bat; he is described as a large animal whose weapon for
killing resembles a burnt staff hardened by fire. While the hero
Hunahpu is peering up out of the mouth of his blowgun to see if
day has dawned, Camazotz flies down and decapitates him. "The
one called *Xecotovach* [a bird of prey] came and gouged out their
eyes; *Camazotz* came and cut off their heads; *Cotzbalam* came and
devoured their flesh" (Goetz and Morley 1950:90).

The sign for night, *akbal*, sometimes occurs on the bat glyph,
just above its eye like a lid. Seler (1909) suggests that it may also
be a symbol for dark thunderclouds. Likewise, Thompson (1966)
remarks on the frequency of the *cauac* glyph, which can be either
infixed or postfixed to the bat. This combination is the site emblem
of Copan (see illustration at beginning of chapter). The bat with
cauac infix also occurs without the emblem affixes. The *cauac* sym-

bol has various meanings, in particular, storms, rain, and lightning.
Seler (1909) points out that *caok* among the Cakchiquel and *cauac*
in Yucatán seem to be interchangeable with a word meaning storm
among the Pokonchi; Stoll has recorded *cahok* as lightning. Čauk is
still used today as a word for storm, thunder, and lightning among
the Maya tribes of Chiapas. In addition, Thompson (1966) notes

that the stucco bat-god modeled on the pyramid at Acanceh as well as the seated bat on the side of the bat-god, have rings around their eyes, such as those worn by the *Tlalocs*, or Mexican rain gods, and both display *Kan* crosses.[3]

In passing, I should mention a few other associations of the bat. Thompson suggests that the *cauac* glyph probably has the phonetic value [ku kul], and he notes that a few bat glyphs have the color affix for red, others for black, and some (rare) glyphs at Palenque would suggest red or great bats (*chac* means both "red" and "large"). In their writings, Heinrich Berlin, John Eric Thompson, and Tatiana Proskouriakoff have commented on the inverted bat glyph. According to Thompson (1966), it is a metamorphogram indicating rest and termination of a period. This is one way of using a symbol and its attributes, in this case, the habit that bats have of sleeping upside down. The metaphor still exists today and an entry in the Aulie and Aulie (1951) Palencano-Chol-English vocabulary reads *'Zutz'atax i wut* for "very tired," or "heavy-headed" (literally "very bat his face").

Given its connection with darkness and rain, the bat's association with fire and the sun seems strange, so strange that Thompson wonders if those instances where the bat glyph follows the sun glyph are not a fortuitous juxtaposition. Yet, there are cases where the sun glyph is actually infixed in the bat glyph; other evidence also indicates that this association is more than chance. Zotzilha Chimalcan, whose image is the bat, is the Cakchiquel god who controls fire. In the *Popol Vuh* there is a group with this symbol that "stole the fire." The answer may be that the bat is not just associated with the light but is also opposed to it; Seler suggests that perhaps the bat glyph is "swallowing" the sun. In a carving at Copan, the bat deity is depicted doing battle with Kukulcan, god of light (Dieseldorff,

---

[3] These crosses have to do with Maya rain symbolism.

1904). Furthermore, one must consider the bat's association with sacrifice and the connection of sacrifice and sun.

There are other flying creatures in Mayan mythology that exhibit this connection with both sun/light/fire and sacrifice. Kinich Kakmo is the "sun-face-fire-macaw" who sends down rays to consume sacrifices made to him (mentioned by Cogulludo in 1868, and in *The Book of Chilam Balam of Chumayel*). Also, some interplay is going on between *zotzil* and *cakix* ("macaw"); in the *Legends of the Cakchiquels* the Zotzils supposedly insisted that "only in the beak of the macaw" could they live and be safe, and so they were called *cakix*. According to Seler (1909), the butterfly was a symbol of fire for the ancient Mexicans. Following Sahagun's narrative, he says that dead warriors are transformed into hummingbirds, flower birds, and butterflies; the latter descend to the earth to suck honey from flowers. Seler and especially Robert Laughlin (from his work among the Tzotzil Maya) identify the flower with sacrifice; Laughlin (1962) treats the flower as a symbol for blood and the forces

of life, including day, the sun, and prosperity. Seler (1909) connects the pointed beak of the hummingbird with a sacrificial instrument. Seler also points out that a special mark of the hummingbird, usually placed on the side of its bill, consists of a small circle surrounded by dots. This sign resembles that of *kak* ("fire"), which appears as the characteristic element in the representation of fire. "But that the bird . . . is in fact connected with sacrifice and boring out the eye as a sign of sacrifice is shown by the Codex Tro example in which are illustrated pre–New Year ceremonies for *cauac* years." In the upper section, Seler (1909) sees a penitent sitting in a dark field surround by pedunculated eyes.

So far then, the connotations of the bat in Mesoamerica have to do with death and sacrifice, in particular with decapitation and extracting the heart, with blood, and, by extension, with flowers and the sun. The bat is connected with the underworld, night, and darkness; he may also be linked with dark clouds, storms, and rain. Probably, its connections with the sun, light, and fire are by way of opposition. In addition, the bat falls into two categories of winged creatures:

1. Those associated with sacrifice and gouged-out eyes—the bat, the hummingbird, and the vulture.

2. Those connected with blood and sacrifice but also with sun and fire and perhaps flowers—the bat, the macaw, the hummingbird, and the butterfly.

If this connection between bats, hummingbirds, and butterflies and the kind of equation made here between flower and sacrificial victim, nectar, and blood, seem tenuous, it might be useful to look at some Maya texts that do not make much sense otherwise, and to consider one adaptation of the bat to its Central American habitat. A passage in the *Book of Chilam Balam of Chumayel* (Roys 1967) reads, "Then descended the four mighty supernatural jars, this was the honey of the flowers." The more intelligible Tizimin (and also the Mani) versions read, "then descended two mighty demon bats who sucked the honey of the flowers" (Makemson 1951). In an article on the flower symbol in Tzotzil beliefs, Laughlin (1962a) comments on the Maya concept of man as a receptacle for blood and suggests a comparison with flowers and their nectar. As both Gates and Thompson (1962) point out, *hunahpu* means "flower." If we reconsider the *Popol Vuh* in which Camazotz beheads Hunahpu, a strange pattern emerges of bats that attack flowers.

Here we have both bats and hummingbirds as sacrificers, their victim being a flower. Thompson mentions that the blood diet of the vampire *Desmodus* is chiefly responsible for the identification of the bat symbol with death, blood, and sacrifice; although he includes the leaf-nosed species in his "composite" bat—as he must, since this feature typifies the glyph—he never discusses *their* diet. In the case of some leaf-nosed bats, of the subfamily *Glossophaginae*, especially the *Glossophaga soricina*—an abundant and widespread species in Middle America—flower nectar is their main food. In a 1932 paper, an Austrian botanist, Otto Porsch, discussed the phenomenon of "batflowers"; these are a group of tropical plants dependent for fertilization on bats that visit the flowers by night in search of nectar or pollen. Porsch mentions several that are common in the Maya area:

Calabash Tree
   (Crescentia)

Silk-Cotton Tree
   (Ceiba and Bombax)

Century Plant
   (Agave)

and other night-blooming cacti of Central America and Mexico

In Chiapas, the crescentia grows only in areas of seasonal swamp, but ceiba grows up in the mountains (Wagner 1964), along with the agaves.

Not only do bats suck nectar, as do hummingbirds, but bat and hummingbird are also found feeding from the same flower. Bat flowers of tropical America "open only at night, but nevertheless are somewhat visited toward evening by hummingbirds . . . At about half-past five in the afternoon the flowers commence to open and reach the height of blossoming in the early hours of night while bats are active, closing again at early dawn" (Allen 1962:116). As Porsch describes them, the bats were much more "nervous" in their actions than hummingbirds. "Darting like arrows, they would alight momentarily on a blossom, clinging to the outer part of the corolla and dipping their heads quickly within, and as quickly dart away" (Allen 1962:117). Given these similarities, it is not surprising that bats—the kind with long extensile tongues for sucking nectar—and hummingbirds might be linked. Perhaps the uncertain light of early evening confused the two in the imaginations of Maya observers.

Let us look at a passage in the *Chilam Balam of Tizimin*: "Sweet was the ancient fruit and succulent on the tongue; sweet to soften the hard heart, to mollify the angry passions, *Chac Vayab* the Bat, he who sucks honey from the flowers" (Makemson 1951). The name *Chac Vayab* suggests still another characteristic attributed to the flower-foraging bat. As will be discussed in a later chapter, both bats and hummingbirds are considered transforming animals in the contemporary Maya world. Roys (1933) points out that the word *vayab* may derive from *vaay*, which in the Motul dictionary is translated as "the familiar of sorcerers"; *vayken* is translated as "sorcerer," or "wizard." I am suggesting that, as the hummingbird and bat gave way to each other at the feeding ground, it might have occurred to observers that one changed into the other and that it is to this quality of transformation, attached to nectar-feeding creatures, that the *Chilam Balam of Tizimin* refers: "Now the wizards vie with one another in taking the shapes of the blue heron and the hummingbird. Then flowers descend from the source and from the folds of the hand nine flowers. When the hearts of the flowers appear the priests place four branches of flowers on the burning altar of the sun."

It is not possible to understand the bat symbol in isolation from other symbols; since there seems to be a real connection between bat and flower, both in nature and in mythology, it would be productive to look at other instances of the flower in Maya material. As Laughlin (1962) suggests, the flower may be a symbol of blood, or, as some of the Maya texts seem to suggest, the "heart of the flower" may be "the heart of the victim," its nectar his blood; at any rate, there is some equivalence between flower and what is sacrificed. Two other connections of flower have to do with fertility. The first is associated with eroticism. The Motul dictionary translates *nicte*, a flower, as "carnal vice" (*vicio de carne*). In a note to the text of *Ritual of the Bacabs* on *Dzunun-Nicte* (hummingbird-plumeria), Roys (1965) points out that the *nicte* (here, plumeria) figures prominently in Maya literature as a symbol for eroticism. The second connection has to do with the sun. In a tale, that seems to have quite ancient roots, reported by Thompson for Belize (British Honduras), the sun falls in love with a girl and wins her by turning himself into a hummingbird and descending to earth to suck the honey of the flowers. In Mexican mythology, the god of flowers *is* the sun, and, as Thompson (1932) points out, the Mayan four-petalled glyph for sun looks like a flower. The bat falls into still a third category:

3. That of sky-diving, nectar-sucking creatures associated with flowers, sun and eroticism, which includes the bat and the hummingbird.

A burial vase from Chamá portrays the exaggerated testicles of the bat-demon, which suggests that he may have had erotic associations. I have found no archaeological evidence, however, that suggests what the mechanism of this connection might be beyond the indirect evidence that relates the bat to flowers and to the sun. In nature, bats enter caves singly and emerge in hordes, and although this habit might create speculation about the extraordinary potency of bats, the fact remains that they are not greatly productive. Normally, females give birth to one baby at a time; breeding is rarely witnessed. The mythical *hʔikʼal*, whom I identify with the bat, is also notoriously potent, but again there is no explanation. As was suggested, the hummingbird, and, according to Thompson (1932), the vulture suggest eroticism. Laughlin provides wonderful corroboration from contemporary Zinacanteco beliefs. If a woman has an illegitimate child, it is remarked that the buzzard's shadow passed over her. To assure himself of sexual prowess while courting, a man will kill a hummingbird and carry it with him. Of a deflowered virgin, men will say, "She was ruined by the bat" (personal communication). In the next section, I will discuss the association of the bat with rain, which seems also to imply the notion of fertility.[4]

3. The Local Bat

One danger in such an archaeological treatment of symbols is that the wrong range can be ascribed to a particular attribute; the derived model could suggest a wider distribution than actually existed. For instance, the bat-tiredness metaphor does not occur in Yucatec Maya, and an inverted bat glyph there (if it exists at all) might mean something very different than it does at geographically nearby Palenque.

The connection between bats and storms (via the *cauac* glyphs, etc.) was probably widespread, occurring as far afield as Chiapas, Yucatán, and Copan, but perhaps the product of this association was different. In Yucatán, the *chac* rain gods appear to have taken on special importance, due to either ecological or historical reasons, or perhaps both. The principal gods of the Yucatec book of *Chilam Balam of Tizimin* include Kukulcan ("he who causes the flowers to open") and the four chacs, who stretched out the earth and planted trees at the cardinal points. In Yucatán, drums and flowers play a part in the rain ceremony held to invoke the *chacs*. These drums, which are called in Mexican *teponaxtli* ("hollow tree"), are connected with the hollow ceiba tree, a symbol of rain (Laughlin 1963).

In view of this ceremonial context, it is possible that the ritual treatment of the bat that I will suggest was unique to Yucatán. Unfortunately, the fact that I did not find any evidence elsewhere does not necessarily mean anything; perhaps no evidence survived or was recorded, or else it was not found by me. In Yucatán, rain was asso-

---

[4] The connection between bats and eroticism certainly occurs in the European version of vampires: "Le vampire . . . est avant tout une creation erotique." (Volta 1962:9).

ciated with the blood of sacrifices, with flowers, and with fertility. The *Tizimin* reads: "When the sealed *katun* was opened immediately the eyes of the Lord opened wide when they saw to the accompaniment of throbbing drums that we were requited by the clearing asunder of the heavens and the descent of the flowers of life, the flowers of rain"; and elsewhere: "Shining were the faces of the Lords of Heavens who were on the point of entering . . . the sweet-smelling heavens, they are agitated by the drums." The description of coming rain suggests that this passage may have had to do with bats: "They are agitated by the drums, the bat is awakened by the drums, the four Bacabs ride to earth on the back of a rainbow."

It may be that I am overly impressed with the "slip" in the *Chumayel* passage, "then descended the four mighty supernatural jars" which elsewhere reads "mighty demon bats" (see page 64)—and with the fact that in Yucatán jars were one representation of the *chacs* who bring rain (Thompson 1966). Just as speculation, I will hazard the image those *Tizimin* passages evoke in my imagination. It once happened that I disturbed some roosting bats. The ensuing chaos was frightening, to say the least. Could this chaos be the source of the *Tizimin* image of waking bats with drums? But why drums? I think the ceremony derives from the habit that bats (which are associated with storms, darkness, and clouds) have of roosting in the hollow ceiba tree, the symbol of rain and also the prototype of the hollow *teponaxtli* drum of the sort used at San Sebastian. This discussion is very speculative, but what does emerge is a bat symbol with local emphases, associated with drums and with some kind of Yucatec ceremony having to do with rain.

4. *H*ʔ*ik'al* and *Soƫ*ʔ

Superficially, there is some connection between *h*ʔ*ik'al* and bats. Both are black, both live in caves,[5] both are considered scavenger robbers associated with blood. The *h*ʔ*ik'al* has

---

[5] People of San Pedro Chenalhó today claim that they find the skeletons of *ʔik'al* (*h*ʔ*ik'al*) in the caves around their village (Guiteras-Holmes 1961: 189). A cache of bat skeletons was found by Richetson along with the bones of small rodents and a bird underneath a stone slab on an altar in the Petén, Guatemala (Allen 1967:22).

wings attached to his feet, and, to some extent, the same could be said of bats. Also, both creatures are anomalous. Black-man, who is possibly a cannibal and apparently ignorant of correct behavior, is neither man nor animal, neither social nor entirely anti-social. He longs for human company and is constantly petitioning the saints to give him someone to talk to—yet this protestation disguises murderous intentions. *H'ik'al* is attracted to fire, but also opposed to it, since it is usually the agent of his destruction. If any animal can be considered anomalous (see chaper 4), the bat can. Bats are furry mammals who give birth to live young, yet they also fly like birds. The bat is further singled out for special treatment by being nocturnal, by living in dark places (caves and hollow trees), by sleeping upside down, and by having the blood-diet of the vampire.

The Tzotzil are fascinated by anomalous animals. While creatures like the jaguar and the dog receive special attention in their folklore, and while stuffed squirrels, monkeys (all anomalous—see next chapter) are given a special place in ritual, the bat is not even mentioned. Yet, as will be discussed later, the Tzotzil are highly aware of his specialness as a "transforming animal." The other creatures in this classification—armadillo, buzzard, butterfly, and hummingbird—are mentioned, and the buzzard and hummingbird at least are frequent protagonists. Nevertheless, certain tales about *h'ik'al* involve descriptions that are surprisingly bat-like.

Sometimes, *h'ik'al* is described as blind or as having bared teeth. Elsewhere he comes "whooshing down like a buzzard." Once, when he was attracted to a campfire, *h'ik'al* is described as follows: "Gliding along he arrived, carried by the wind . . . He landed at the foot of a big tree . . . (when the men awoke) he was squatting at their fireside" (RML, tale 126). Sometimes *h'ik'al* resembles a cat (RML, tale 127). The following passage describes raids made by *h'ik'al* on a Zinacanteco henhouse:

Oh the spook knocked on the door. He knocked on the boards. He kept picking up the hens . . . He shook the chickens from the peach tree . . . The woman noticed when it dawned the next day that the hens were lying about, some of them wounded. [On the second night] the same

thing happened. But now it was the dog he hit. They had a pig. He came
and pulled their pig along . . . "But, man, our pig has gone!" [the
woman said] . . .

When it dawned after the second night they saw a puddle of blood
by the door . . . The dog was curled up [by the stile] asleep. But one of
its ears was hurt.[6] You see it was because [the spook] had cut off its ear.
Who knows what use it was to him (RML, tale 127).

It is the habit of bats to return to the same location night after
night, but in no text that I examined does *hʔik'al* behave this way.
As far as I know there is no other reference to *hʔik'al* wounding
chickens or attacking pigs. It may be that *hʔik'al* makes the pigs too
nervous to move normally (as they would be if they sensed the presence of a vampire?). There is the evidence left the next day, the
"pool of blood." The language of this passage suggests some kind
of slip; or perhaps the storyteller was opening up, dropping his
usual camouflage, and expanding on characteristics of *hʔik'al* normally left unspoken.

An interview between E. Z. Vogt and his informant Chep Her-
nandez Perez (personal communication 1968) indicates the pres-
sures that might motivate this camouflage. Chep says: "The bat is
called *ʔanhel*. The old people say you can't say the name *tsots* [*soʦ'*—
the bat which comes to suck blood] because if you do, he will come
and suck more blood. Instead you should say *ʔanhel* came to suck
blood—then the bat won't come anymore . . ."

Similarly, in San Pedro Chenalhó, terms referring to evil creatures are avoided in several situations. The Tzotzil informant Manuel describes a former time when there were many dangers: "We
could not say the word *'ik'al* [*hʔik'al*] because they would hear it
and come to get us. They would be referred to as *natil kaxlan* ['High
Master']" (Guiteras-Holmes 1961:189). There, the euphemizing
term *ʔanhel*, or "throne of *ʔanhel*," is reserved for snakes that are
feared. Snakes are also called "his pets" or "his hummingbirds"
(Guiteras-Holmes 1961:303).

Interesting possibilities are raised by the use of the term *ʔanhel*.
If the current Maya Black-man is a manifestation of the ancient bat,
further corroboration would be provided for the bat's association

[6] The dog with a torn ear is a recurrent theme in ancient Mexico (Seler 1909).

with rain. According to Villa-Rojas (personal communication to Vogt) and Vogt (1969:302) the name ?*anhel* is a corruption of the ancient Maya *canhel*, the staff carried by certain gods and god-impersonators; it is associated with rain and winds. Robert Laughlin (personal communication) suggests that the name ?*anhel*, which is substituted for "bat," may also include some reference to the "earth lord." In San Pedro Chenalhó, the term ?*anhel* does mean "rain god" (see Guiteras-Holmes 1961, glossary definitions), though it is used there as a euphemism for snakes rather than for bats. I wonder, however, if there is not some connection between the Pedrano "High Master" (*h?ik'al*) and the Zinacanteco ?*anhel*, "earth lord" (bat).

H?ik'al himself provides further evidence by the company he keeps and by behavior consistent with the ancient bat-demon's. In San Pedro Chenalhó there is a strange antagonism at work between Black-man and the hummingbird. "All the *wayhels* [*vayihel* "animal souls"] tried in the struggle against '*ik'al* [*h?ik'al*]. The hummingbird—*ts'unun* [*ṫ'unun*] was the bravest of all . . . because it was he who vanquished the enemies of man." The weapons of the hummingbird are flaming arrows that are "like fire," for he is a sun creature as opposed to the nocturnal ones:

Everyone knows about the *Totilmeil* [*totil me?il*; ancestors, or else one who has the hummingbird as his animal soul] because it was he who destroyed the . . . '*ik'al* [*h?ik'al*] . . . The people would have to close themselves in their homes by four or five in the afternoon. And that is when the *Totilmeil* [*totil me?il*] appeared. The nocturnal birds gathered together with the fox, the jaguar, the owl, but the hummingbird won over all of them (Guiteras-Holmes 1961:263).

Similarly, in ancient times the hummingbird was a creature identified with the sun and the forces of life. It may be that the bat glyph appears in connection with the sun, opposed to it or swallowing it. Both are sky-diving creatures linked to flowers and sacrifice.

At the Zinacanteco fiesta of San Sebastian, *h?ik'al* is the entertaining colleague of *bolom* (Jaguar) and *k'uk'ul čon*—two apparent carry-overs from classic Maya times. Furthermore, *h?ik'al* as he is described in myths from San Pedro Chenalhó resembles

Camazotz, bat-demon of the *Popol Vuh*. There, Black-men supposedly carry people off to their caves (where they live in a village
called Papasalenco) and behead them. A charting of these parallels
reads as follows:

Ancient times:
　　Camazotz beheads Hunahpu
　　Demon-bat takes honey from flowers
In Nature:
　　Bat sucks nectar from flowers
San Pedro today:
　　hʔik'al beheads human victims

From these ethnographic accounts it is apparent that ancient
Maya deities have been retained intact to some extent: the hummingbird—with its connotations of sun and ancestors—the jaguar,
k'uk'ul čon, and so on. Along with these we would expect to find
the bat, since the bat symbol was widespread in ancient times and
since anomalous reminders of the bat are constantly present in
nature. It is nowhere to be found in current folktales, however,
unless it is in the form of *hʔik'al*. Even though *hʔik'al* may have
absorbed many characteristics from an ancient prototype, he also
continues to absorb traits that are consistent with his myth-nature.
For instance, when Negro workers were brought into Chiapas to
build roads, the Tzotzil were reported to be afraid of them. Perhaps
the black man seemed fearsome because he resembled one trait-type
of *hʔik'al* (blackness). Once the two were identified, it is easy to
see how curly hair, an unbatlike trait, might be ascribed to *hʔik'al*.

The following chart attempts to summarize the connotations of
the ancient bat symbol. It covers a wide timespan, from 300 A.D.
until the period after the Spanish Conquest, as well as a wide geographical range, from scattered North Mexican examples to Honduras. The bat symbol emerges from this generalized scheme as
a complicated cluster of symbols and connotations. The problem
that remains concerns the legitimacy of extrapolating from these
scattered sources to a discussion of the specific nature of the bat-
demon as it existed in the mind of any one individual. I do not
know a good answer, but I do believe that some of these traits—
for instance the demon's association with death, blood, and sex-

uality—are core connotations that are both widespread and constant connotations of the symbol.

Death	Sacrifice	Darkness
rest	plucked-out eyes	black
termination of a period	decapitation	cold
sleeping upside down	hearts plucked out	night
		underworld
		clouds

Forces of Life	Blood	Eroticism	Rain
	Flowers	Sun	fertility
		light	hollow ceiba
		fire	beating drums

In addition to its thematic associations the bat symbol shares connotations with other animal symbols. Apparently, attributes may also be exchanged between related symbols:

Vulture—black, scavenger
        —sacrifice—plucks out eyes and heart
        —eroticism

Hummingbird—creature that sucks flowers
                —sacrifice—heart, nectar, blood, and forces of life
                —light, sun, and fire
                —eroticism

Macaw—light, sun, and fire

Butterfly—fire
        —flowers

iv. Anomalous Animals

'Mother, [said the Baby Jaguar] there are two new animals in the woods today, and the one you said couldn't swim [hedgehog] swims and the one that you said couldn't curl up [tortoise] curls; and they've gone shares in their prickles, I think because both of them are scaly all over, instead of one being smooth and the other very prickly; and besides that, they are rolling round and round in circles, and I don't feel comfy.' Mother Jaguar answers: 'A hedgehog is a hedgehog and can't be anything but a hedgehog and a tortoise is a tortoise and can never be anything else . . . but it isn't a hedgehog and it isn't a tortoise. It's a little of both, and I don't know its proper name.' They are speaking of an armadillo (Kipling 1929).

N*agualism*[1] is one of the most complex topics in Middle American mythology. The concept is so widespread, and the term so subject to local interpretations, that I do not have the courage to deal with it here.[2] Nevertheless, it is important to remember that the ties between animals and men in the Maya area are more

[1] Originally perhaps, the term *nagual* was applied only to transforming witches. Molina's dictionary (1571) translates the word as *bruxa* (Foster 1944:88–89).

[2] "In Mexico and Guatemala the word *nagualism* has . . . been used as a convenient container into which . . . [one] could dump a variety of magical beliefs and practices which among themselves show considerable variation and no necessary relationships" (Foster 1944:103). See also Saler 1967.

complicated than most Westerners can imagine. A man has a permanent soul and an animal soul. In addition, there are animal forms a witch can take, animal forms a witch controls, and special animals a witch guards. Along with the innocent animals that roam the paths, there are supernaturally charged animals that come from the mountain. All co-exist and interrelate and have deeper connotations for a Maya than they do to us.

In general, *espantos* can be divided into those that turn into animals and those that merely behave in a non-human way, or that share in animal attributes without actually taking on animal form. At first glance, *hʔik'al*, a permanently inhuman black demon, suits the second description. However, if *hʔik'al* really is a kind of unnamed symbol or euphemism for the bat-demon, he would also fit into the class of spooks with animal forms—with the qualification that he does not change shape. Usually, the animal vehicles for these spooks are creatures that fit Douglas' definition of anomalous beings —they defy culturally dictated categories or are classifiable into more than one category.

These ambiguous animals crop up in several contexts where anomalies are being dealt with—for example, they appear as stuffed animals at San Sebastian. In this chapter I discuss these anomalous animals as well as a group of animals that are anomalous with a special twist; these are transforming animals who change from one animal to another.

1. What Constitutes an Amomalous Animal?

Douglas describes the pangolin,[3] a cult symbol of the Lele of Central Africa, as a being contradicting "all the most obvious animal categories. It is scaly like a fish, but it climbs trees. It is more like an egg-laying lizard than a mammal, yet it suckles its young" (1966:168–169). In her doctoral thesis, "Laughter in Zinacantan," Bricker takes this concept of anomaly and applies it to Tzotzil classifications. She believes that some anomalous animals are those which Zinacantecos find analogous to humans in

---

[3] The pangolin is an African animal that looks very much like an armadillo. While armadillos usually have quadruplets, pangolins appear to have only one offspring at a time.

some respect. For instance, Zinacantecos believe that squirrels are like people because they cross themselves as people do. Of the stuffed squirrels used at San Sebastian to represent "shameless women" who are the wives of defaulting cargoholders she says: "What better animal to have represent the wife of an errant religious official than one which seems to make pious gestures! (Bricker 1968:273). Dogs and chickens are anomalous because they are members of no one category but enjoy a position intermediate between pets and yard animals (Bricker 1968).[4]

Zinacantecos makes a clear distinction between animals that live on the wooded slopes of the Chiapas mountains (a zone called *te?tik*) and animals that are common to areas used and controlled by humans (*naetik*)—such as houses, waterholes, and fields (Acheson 1961).[5] This distinction suggests that the concept of anomaly should not be confined to only those animals which resemble people. An animal like the mouse might also be anomalous; it is a "wild" animal, yet it also lives in human houses and eats human food. A line from RML, tale 81, about the charcoal-cruncher indicates that Zinacantecos take special notice of the mouse's habit of gnawing (apparently eating) wood. Obviously, *something* is special about mice. Zinacantecos believe that mice are transforming animals that turn into bats (see next section). Other anomalous animals are dogs and goats, domestic creatures that scavenge for refuse. Dogs are particularly interesting: they live in close proximity to man but are not treated like humans. They are generally despised and kicked about. Often they are starving and eat whatever they can get—including excrement (Acheson 1961).

Animals are anomalous if they fit into both animal and human categories, that is, if they (1) resemble people, or (2) live in human areas and eat human food or refuse. They may be anomalous if they fit into more than one animal category (like Douglas' pangolin). If any animal is anomalous, the bat is. It is a mammalian

---

[4] Her comments are fashioned after Leach's paradigm from a paper on animal imagery and verbal abuse (1964): self (human): house (pet):: yard (livestock): woods (wild).

[5] Literally, *naetik* means "houses," *te?tik* "expanse of trees."

insectivore, which gives birth to live young and nurses them; it has fur, big pointed ears, and a face like a cat,[6] or a mouse—yet it flies and has wings like a bird. Bats eat fruit, or else drink blood or nectar. In Zinacantan, the bat is classified among *pepenetik*, which are winged insects, yet it is also thought to resemble a mouse, since it is a mouse that turns into a bat.

Before passing on to the subject of *hʔikʼal* and the bat and their relation to transforming animals, I would like to return to the subject of the stuffed animals carried at San Sebastian. Both the *bolometik* and *hʔikʼaletik* carry stuffed squirrels and iguanas. The habit that squirrels have of "praying" has been mentioned. Iguanas are tree-living lizards, peculiar perhaps in their own right, but definitely unusual because of their association with chickens. Chickens are domestic animals living in close proximity to man, almost to the point of being pets, yet they are eaten. Normally, their place is in the yard, but when they are going to be sacrificed, chickens are brought inside the house where they become sacrificial substitutes for human beings (Bricker 1968). Iguana flesh tastes like chicken and may be substituted for chicken in ceremonies.

The *bolometik* also carry a coati (called *kotom*). This animal figures in the tree-raising ceremonies of Yucatán (Redfield 1930). Its Yucatec Maya name, *chic*, means buffoon or clown. It is a raccoon-like creature with a long snout. Like the opossum, it has five fingers. Raccoons and opossums are classified by Zinacantecos as animals that stink, and perhaps the coati was included with them in this category—though this is just a guess. The fifth kind of stuffed animal carried by the *hʔikʼal* are spider monkeys. Spider monkeys[7] are rarely seen in the highlands, but Zinacantecos apparently know what they are. The agility in the air of these monkeys may be an important element in their identification. Pictures of flying squirrels shown to Zinacantecos elicited the name *pepen čuč* "bat squirrel,"

[6] In myth, *hʔikʼal* himself is sometimes described as looking like a cat.

[7] Spider monkeys (like squirrel monkeys) have white rings around their eyes; though I know of no evidence to support this, it is possible that the performing *hʔikʼal* with a white mask about his eyes (see picture section) is imitating these monkeys.

or "butterfly squirrel" (personal communication from Nick Acheson).[8]

Monkeys resemble people in build and facial expression, and they have a long tradition in Maya folklore of representing men turned into animals. The *Popol Vuh* version about the men of wood who angered their creator by not speaking is perhaps the most well-known example. In order to punish them, because "they had not thought of their father or mother," all their belongings—their earthen jars, griddles, plates, pots, and grinding stones—plus all the animals of the barnyard, gang up against them and destroy their faces. All of nature turns against them: "The desperate men of wood tried to escape by climbing to the tops of the houses, but the houses fell down; they wanted to climb to the treetops, but trees cast them down; they wanted to enter caverns, but the caves repelled them.

"The mouths and faces of all of them were mangled. Their descendants are the monkeys that now live in the forest.

"And therefore the monkey looks like man." (*Popol Vuh* 1950: part I, chapters 2 and 3). Similarly in a creation myth from Acatán, Guatemala, "Younger Brother" (who is God) shames his brothers by performing a better dance than they do. Then, he offers to show them where he obtained his wonderful costumes. "They went on their way until they arrived at the seat of a very great tree. God told them to climb up; [when] he saw that they had already ascended he went up behind them. The tree continued to grow, going very far up. Then he [God] stripped the bark from the tree, formed a lagoon at the base of the tree, and . . . commanded that once for all they should remain there because they had behaved very badly to him." When the Mother arrives to see what has happened to the brothers, she questions them, "Is it you?" The monkeys shake the tree in reply, and some refuse falls into her eyes. Angered by this, she commands them to remain animals forever. According to the people in San Miguel Acatán, "The monkeys are the Ancient Men,

---

[8] A Central African (Ndembu) folktale about the flying squirrel tells how he tried to live with the birds but was rejected because he had a tail, teeth, and fur, like an animal. Then he tried to live with the animals, but they rejected him because he flew like a bird (Turner 1968:116–117).

the brothers of God's Mother, the Virgin" (Siegal 1943:120–126).

In a Zinacanteco tale about the great flood, the Lord finds a group of survivors who subsisted on vine berries and nuts. He questions them and, when they reply rudely, the Lord tells them to "look at your backsides," and they are turned into monkeys. As one Zinacanteco tells the story, there are two families of humans, people like themselves and others: "Their tails appeared; their ears appeared; their hair; now their faces look like humans. So that they didn't become well-made people . . . they have long hair and long tails because they didn't obey the Lord's order—they went to the woods" (RML, tale 70).

A sailor about to cross the equator for the first time is a 'polywog'; once across, he becomes a 'shell-back.'

(From an article in the Nov. 28, 1969 *San Francisco Examiner*; astronaut Dick Gordon was temporarily christened "Luney-wog.")

2. Transforming Animals

As he is described both in myth (RML, tale 130) and in conversations at San Sebastian,[9] *hʔikʼal* resembles a buzzard. Both are black, winged scavengers; while *hʔikʼal* eats people and (perhaps) cooked blood, the buzzard eats carrion. In myths about a lazy man who turns into a buzzard, *šulem vinik* (RML, tales 42, 48, and 69), the buzzard has a reputation like Black-man's for flying to fire.[10] This belief may derive from actual observation of the buzzard, since birds of prey are frequently seen circling above the scene of grass fires. They are attracted not to the fire but to mice and other small game flushed by the flames. In addition, the buzzard may be associated with *hʔikʼal* by virtue of

[9] The joking Alfereces distribute cigarettes and tell the Black-men that they are buzzards and not Black-men because they seem to have wings (Bricker 1965–1966 Fieldnotes: text 958).

[10] RML, tale 126 and EZV F-1:8—*hʔikʼal* crouched by fire eating; RML, tale 127—*hʔikʼal*'s victim is "burning," he comes to put out "fire"; RML, tales 67 and 71—woman victim is asleep by fire, *hʔikʼal* is scalded and/roasted.

his anomalousness. Zinacantecos believe that a buzzard "stinks" like a man who has been working. Strangely, in Zinacantan and in San Pedro la Laguna this characteristic bad odor, "a smell like a buzzard," is attributed to laziness. The fact that some spooks also stink—the *characotel* in San Pedro la Laguna (Rosales 1949:430) is said to have "olor como zopilote"—suggests that this may be an anomalous attribute equivalent to bloodshot eyes, shaggy hair, and so on.

Other animals which, according to Zinacantecos, stink are the red fox, the raccoon, the opossum,[11] the skunk, the jaguar, and the coyote (Bricker 1968:171). In fact, several, perhaps all, of these animals do have a strong smell. At any rate the skunk, opossum, and coyote do, and it may be significant that bats, the prototype for *hʔikʼal*, also smell. Bats are provided with scent glands that emit a strong, musky odor meant to attract female bats, but it is easily detectable by humans (Allen 1962:138). These glands are stimulated by any kind of excitement, and when a bat is frightened or caught this odor becomes very obvious after a while. Furthermore, a cave or hollow tree used by bats as a retreat for any length of time begins to smell from their droppings—so much so, that this odor may be detectable from a considerable distance (Allen 1962:69–70 and 138).

The association of *hʔikʼal* with the buzzard may also reflect the fact that in Zinacantan both the buzzard and the bat, as well as the hummingbird, are transforming animals. For the Tzotzil Maya of Zinacantan, the bat *sotʼ* is classified with *pepenetik*, a category of winged insects and butterflies. They say, "es rata pero va como *pepen* ["butterfly"] o pájaro," the criterion here being large wings (Acheson 1962). Undoubtedly, they consider the bat anomalous; it is a mouse, *yašal čʼo*, or *lumtikil čʼo*, that has turned itself into a flying thing. According to the Tzotzil, when a mouse grows old, it goes to a deserted path in the woods. If it can jump successfully

---

[11] In this section I discuss the transforming animals, bat, buzzard, and hummingbird, but the opossum too is believed to have changed its shape. Originally it was a human. This origin is reflected in its five fingers (Bricker 1968:172). It may be significant that Zinacantecos say when an animal with five toes is killed, it is *čanul*; if it has only four toes, then it is not a *čanul* ("animal soul").

Nectar-sipping bat (photo by Bruce Hayward)

Bolometik and *b'ik'taletik* on the Bolom Te (stuffed animals represent wives of cargoholders)

Bolom climbing the Bolom Te

H ʔik'aletik and *bolometik* throwing stuffed animals from the jaguar tree

Bolometik and *b ʔik'al* throwing food from Bolom Te

H ʔikʰal grabbing young bystanders at the fiesta of San Sebastian

¢onteʔ covered with Spanish moss

four times from one side of the path to the other, it turns into a bat and flies away. Like the bat, the butterfly is transformed from a ground-living thing, the *ɫukum* (caterpillar), into a flying creature, *pepen*.

The hummingbird (*k'oɔol pepen*) and the turkey-buzzard (*ɫahal niʔ šulem*) share with *soɔ'* this quality of transformation. *K'oɔol pepen* is a hummingbird with a white head and body that was once a butterfly; Zinacantecos believe that the change takes place sometime in the beginning of August. The word *k'oɔol* refers to this change.[12] *Ȼahal niʔ* šulem is believed to be a very old armadillo that has gone into a cave and starved itself until, on the verge of dying, it sprouts wings and flies away (Acheson 1962). Hummingbirds and butterflies are fairly obvious "relatives," and the similarity between mice and bats is certainly recognized in many parts of the world (compare German *Fledermaus*, French *chauve-souris*, our Webster's "any of a number of related mouselike mammals . . ."). The connection between armadillos and turkey-buzzards is, however, particularly queer. The two species of buzzard common to Middle America are the turkey vulture, *Cathartes aura*, and the black vulture, *Coragyps atratus*. Perhaps the bald, scaly head of the turkey-vulture suggests that of the armadillo, or it may be that, like the vulture, the armadillo is regarded as "special" for similar reasons. This "specialness" would relate the two. Probably the armadillo referred to is the common nine-banded armadillo, *Dasypus novemcinctus*, by reputation a very good animal to eat (Stuart 1964:318).

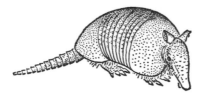

Armadillos live in burrows and have the remarkable adaptation of holding their breath while digging furiously. Armadillos have

[12] There are approximately 319 species of hummingbird in Middle America, and, although the majority are restricted to the lowlands, hummingbirds are found at all elevations. One genus (*Selasphorus*) is confined to the highlands (Stuart 1964:323).

tough armor plates, and when in danger they can roll themselves up into an almost invulnerable ball. Nevertheless, they are also speedy runners. Armadillos feed mostly on insects and small reptiles; if need be, however, they eat carrion (Dorst 1967:127) and this fact may be critical in the Zinacanteco connection between the armadillo and the turkey-vulture.

As was pointed out in chapter 3, some leaf-nosed bats (subfamily *Glossophaginae*) join hummingbirds at twilight as the former suck nectar from the flowers. A strange passage from Nick Acheson's fieldnotes underscores the similarity between bats and hummingbirds in the Zinacanteco view. The informant Domingo de la Torre Perez is talking about *smayol*, one of the *ts'ununetik* (*ʄ'ununetik* "hummingbirds") that flies and sings only at night. *Smayol* is also a transformed butterfly, but Domingo provides no description. In fact, it may be that *smayol* is invisible. *Smayol* is a messenger of the ancestor gods (*totil-meʔitik*), though others of the nocturnal hummingbirds, called *sts'unun h'ak chamel* (*ʄ'unun h'ak'-čamel*), are thought to carry sickness from the witches (Acheson 1962:66).[13] *Smayol's* characteristic song is a short, disconnected "ts', ts', ts'." Domingo actually remembers a night occasion when this creature flew overhead several times, emitting high short chirps at regular intervals. He tried to see it with his flashlight but could not.[14] To me, this creature sounds like a bat.

Like the word *zotz* (*soʄ'*) for bat, that for butterfly, *pepen, pepem,* or *pehpem* (*zulepor k'ek zulup* in Highland Guatemala), is widespread in the Maya area (Seler 1909), but I do not know whether these and the other transforming animals of Zinacantan are regarded as transformers. Around Lake Atitlán, at Panajachel[15] (Tax 1950:688) and at San Pedro la Laguna (Rosales 1950:636), the belief exists that the bat is a transformed mouse.

[13] Elsewhere, in San Juan Chamelco bats are creatures sent by witches to carry sickness (Carrera 1949:126).

[14] The son of one of Laughlin's storytellers claims to have seen the evil hummingbird; it was black and pullet-sized (personal communication from Robert Laughlin).

[15] An interesting belief exists in Panajachel about bats who smoke. If you catch one put a lighted cigarette in its mouth and it will smoke "como hace la gente" (Tax 1950:688).

In Tzotzil eyes at least, there is a special status ascribed to animals that change their shape. Evidence from San Pedro Chenalhó emphasizes this and indicates that these animals comprise a special group. One creature in that group automatically suggests another. Guiteras-Holmes' informant Manuel discusses transforming animals. The *okinahual* "has four tiny legs near its head; the head is black and it has two teeth; without tail or hair or wings; little eyes on either side of the head; it doesn't jump, it is inside the tree trunk like a baby rat; it turns into a butterfly and then it will have wings, spotted blue and looking like silk . . . *'Uch* [opossum and also a small unidentified insect believed to eat the strength of the food] is greatly respected because it has fire, . . . if it is not respected . . . the crop will be poor and we will go hungry."

Guiteras-Holmes next tells us that Manuel thinks "spontaneously" of the bat. "The bat is dangerous, it is evil. The bat resembles *Tentación* [the devil] because it can change its shape" (Guiteras-Holmes 1961:196–197).

A curious taboo exists also in San Pedro against eating the *xcumob*, an animal associated with approaching rain, with clouds, and with lightning. Whenever the water dries up, an animal called *k'onon* is believed to sprout wings and to fly. It then becomes a *xcumob*. The reason for not eating this creature is that it has changed its shape (Guiteras-Holmes 1961:197). This subject of food taboo deserves more attention than I can give it here. For instance, an armadillo is *called* a turkey in San Pedro so that it *can* be eaten.[16] Could this be related to the armadillo in Zinacantan that becomes a turkey-buzzard? If so how? (Buzzards are not eaten either.)

In the case of the bat and the turkey-vulture, the trend seems to be transformation from a ground-living animal into a flying creature. In the case of the hummingbird, however, it seems to be one flying thing (a butterfly) turning into another flying thing. Nevertheless, by going back one stage in the development of a butterfly, to when this creature was a *ţukum* ("caterpillar"), this distinction is overcome.

[16] "Some wild animals cannot be eaten unless they . . . are changed into others; this is accomplished by speaking to them under a different name. The rabbit, here, and field rat are called deer; the armadillo is called a turkey, the gopher is called a wild boar. The jaguar is never mentioned" (Guiteras-Holmes 1961:303).

ground				*air*
mouse	→			bat
armadillo	→			turkey-buzzard
caterpillar	→	butterfly	→	hummingbird

Animals that are anomalous to start with, or whose identity is sometimes ambiguous (the confusion between the butterfly and the bat), are placed in a more complicated framework that is associated with both ground and air habitats.

Interestingly, these three air-borne transformers, the bat, the buzzard, and the hummingbird, are all sky-diving creatures anciently connected with sacrifice and gouged-out eyes (see previous chapter). In addition, the bat and the hummingbird (as well as the butterfly) were associated with blood, perhaps with flowers, and with fire by the ancient Maya. Bats may be further associated with hummingbirds because of their similar habits and their common diet of flower nectar. Among the Maya, where flowers have special significance as symbols for blood and the forces of life (see p. 66), a connection with flowers would be an impressive facet of any creature associated with sacrifice, and this connection may, of course, have contributed to the association. If such a relation between the hummingbird and the bat persists today, it would lend special significance to the myths about *hʔikʼal* as they are told in San Pedro Chenalhó, where *hʔikʼal* struggles against *tsʼunun* (*ṭʼunun*) "the hummingbird" in a cosmic battle between good and evil (Guiteras-Holmes 1961:248). Though both the hummingbird and the bat were instruments of sacrifice in ancient times, a similar dichotomy may have existed then between good and evil—the hummingbird associated with the sun, the bat with darkness.

The sacrificial connotations of the buzzard persist today in Zinacantan. Bricker (Field data for 1965–1966, text 61, "Buzzard Face") records a tale about a man who falls asleep and whose eyeballs are gouged out by a buzzard. This story is strikingly reminiscent of the ancient vulture who tears out human eyes (Seler 1909). History could explain this parallel, or it could also be the result of common observation. Apparently, it really is the habit of vultures to peck out the eyes first (Stempell 1909:28).

I am fascinated by the idea that creatures like the bat and turkey-vulture, which were associated with death and sacrifice in ancient times, might be connected by Maya today with the concept of vengeance and with the notion of broken norms. In San Pedro la Laguna, a child who urinates in its pants is reprimanded by being told he "stinks" like a buzzard; people who don't wash their feet are likewise told that they have *patas de zopilote* ("buzzard's feet"; Rosales 1949:621). In San Pedro a lazy man is threatened with the admonition that he will turn into a buzzard. Zinacantecos and many other groups in Middle America associate the easy-living, sky-circling buzzard with shirkers. Tales about the lazy man who changes places with the buzzard and who is then burned to death while searching for food are widespread.

Likewise, *hʔikʼal*, whose prototype may be the sacrificing bat (Camazotz who bites off heads, etc.), has the task at San Sebastian of admonishing malefactors—negligent cargoholders and their wives. In chapter 6 I discuss the possible offenses that the female victims of *hʔikʼal* might have committed. The questions that remain are to what extent *hʔikʼal* is held up as a bogie who avenges broken norms and, if he is such a character, what kind of norms are involved.

v. Themes of Anomaly

There is the familiar belief about hags—women who shed their skin and victimize sleepers—'ol' haigs what ride people in de sleep' . . . 'Say if you want to catch dat haig' . . . you must put salt and pepper in the discarded skin (Herskovits 1958; from Georgia Sea Islands).

Structuralism lends itself dangerously to arbitrary analyses. It may be that the facility of the analyst produces more oppositions than are actually present in the myths. An interesting question might be—what motives could occur that are not reducible to oppositions like nature-culture, life-death, male-female? The point, though, is that, where these oppositions occur, there seems to be a balance or interplay between them that could not be haphazard.

Whether the oppositions emerge from the tales themselves or whether they are merely the imposition of a theoretically brainwashed Cambridge mind, it is fantastic how neatly the spook themes fall into place in terms of the contrasts between man and animal, the dead and the live, male and female. Spooks are creatures existing somewhere between these poles, associated with conditions that are likewise ambiguous. A kind of equivalence exists between these anomalies; details in the myths also fill structural oppositions, the

victims they attack are similarily anomalous, and the devices used in destroying spooks are comparably disambiguating.

> There were some newlyweds whose parents were still alive, but she liked to go out at night in the form of a black goat. Her husband found out about it and prepared himself a *chichicaste* stick and a little salt, which was the only thing with which to punish her. One night he felt her catch hold of his nose and go out into the patio. She did a flip [*dar vuelta*] once at the doorway, again in the patio, and a final time at the entrance of the *sitio*. Her husband watched as she changed form and listened as the neighborhood dogs barked at her. He threw salt on the skin which she left behind at the foot of a cross, and then went back to sleep.
>
> When the woman returned and tried to put on her skin, she could not because it had salt on it.
> Carnero-Woman, from Panajachel
> (translated with permission of the
> recorder from Tax 1950:2560)

1. Salt, Garlic, and Tobacco

Zinacantecos define as "human" people who behave according to their social prescriptions; those who deviate from these norms are not "human." Instead they are compared to animals—promiscuous people are compared to pigs and dogs, and lazy people, or people who smell, to buzzards. A man who suspects his wife of eating carrion asks her: "Are you a dog, are you a buzzard, why do you eat corpses?" (RML, tale 4) The kind of criteria being used here emerges from a Zinacanteco tale about a man whose wife turns him into a dog.

THE MAN WHO WAS TURNED INTO A DOG

Once a boy and a girl got married. They acquired many maids. Well, the woman went out every night, but the man didn't hear his wife leave. He thought she just went outside [to go to the bathroom]. It was the same every night. The man noticed it. When he went to bed he had his gun and his machete ready. He didn't fall asleep. At midnight the woman got up. She felt her husband's chest to see whether he was asleep or awake. When she heard that her husband didn't move, she went out at midnight.

The man got up too. He took his gun and his machete. He followed his wife wherever she went. "Could she have a lover?" said the man. "But I'll kill both of them now," he said.

She went, she went very far. She arrived at the cemetery. She arrived to dig [there]. She tried out a corpse. She left it. She went to another and dug it up. Then she found good meat. She ate it. The man was watching from a distance. "Well, never mind. I've seen now what it is she's doing," said the man. "Well, never mind, I'll go back," he said.

He arrived home. He arrived and went to bed. He waited for his wife to return. He looked as if he were asleep. He didn't move. His wife arrived and opened the door. She came to sleep. "Well, where did you go?" he asked his wife.

"I went outside, I went to the bathroom [to urinate]," the woman answered.

"Hell, that's a lovely thing you're doing," he told his wife. Quickly he picked up his machete and hit his wife with the flat of the machete. "How can it be? Are you a dog? Are you a buzzard? Why do you eat corpses?" his wife was asked. Then the woman cried and cried.

The next day her husband suddenly turned into a black dog. The poor dog wasn't given its tortillas. It just ate shit. But it couldn't stand that. It wasn't used to that. The man was familiar with another town. He [used to] go there on his trips. He had a good friend there. "Well, I'm going. I can't stand it. I'm starving," said the dog.

He arrived at a store. He sat down on a chair. There were many newspapers scattered about. The dog looked at them. "But this isn't a dog. He knows how to read," said the storekeeper. The dog was spoken to. "Have you always been a dog?"

"No," he said.

"Are you a human being?"

"Yes," he said. The dog made signs with his head. The lunch hour arrived. They ate. He was given a lot of meat, tortillas, and bread by the storekeeper. The dog was given everything.

An old woman arrived. She came to buy bread. "If you want, we'll go right away."

"Let's go," said the dog. He went with the old woman.

"Have you always been a dog or are you a human being?" she asked.

"Yes [I'm a man]," he answered with his head.

When they arrived at the old woman's house—"Do you want to turn into a human being again?" asked the woman.

"I want to," said the dog. Suddenly he became a human being.

"What happened to you?" he was asked.

"Well, it was my wife who was doing all sorts of things, so I hit her. Because it was like this and this," he said.

Well, the maids missed him. "Mistress," they said, "where is our master?"

"Who knows, maybe he went to look for his girl friend," said the woman.

"Ah," said the maids.

As for that old woman—"What do you think you'll do to her? Do you want to do something to her?" the man was asked.

"Ah, but I don't know how. I'd like to, but I don't know how to do it," he replied.

"Ah, well, if you give me plenty of money I know what to do."

"I'll give it to you," said the man.

"Ah, she and I learned together. She knows less. I'm stronger," said the old woman.

"Please, I'll give you however much you want," said the man.

"Well, all right, we'll see. Go, go into your house," said the old woman.

"Fine, I'm going then. Please, I'll come bring you pay," he said.

"All right, go! She can't do anything to you now."

He arrived home. "Oh, master, you've come back?" said all the maids. "I thought you had died," said the maids.

"No, God doesn't want that. I have returned," he said. Quickly he was given his meal. He ate well. The maids embraced him and kissed him. "Are you here, woman?" he asked his wife.

"I am here. Have you come back?" she said.

"I have come back," he said.

Suddenly the woman turned into a mare. "Look, daughter," the man said to his maids. "What, master?" they said. "Take away the mare. Go tie it in the stall, but let it starve to death. Don't give it its meal, because it has done wrong," said the man. Then, tied up, it starved. Then it grew thin. Then the mare died.

"Where did our mistress go?" the maids asked their master.

"Who knows where she went. Maybe she went to look for another husband."

"Ah," they said. Just so ends the story for now. (RML, tale 4)

The plot shuttles back and forth between situations with a human bias and those with an animal slant. Monogamy, living in a house, having servants, eating tortillas, knowing how to read—all of these are civilized activities. Promiscuity, eating carrion or excrement, starving—all of these pursuits are uncivilized. These themes recur at intervals throughout the tale and seem to provide evidence that the oppositions mentioned above really exist and are not being imposed by the analyst. Table 12 portrays the oppositions present in the above tale.

Table 12. *Oppositions Present in RML, tale 4*

Human	Non-human	
getting married (monogamy)		having a lover (promiscuity)
house with maids		
man eats tortillas	dog eats shit	wife digs for corpses and eats them
	man turns into dog	wife is called "dog," "buzzard," "cabron"
dog goes to town		wife goes to cemetery
dog reads		
dog fed by storekeeper	dog not fed	mare tied in stall and starved
dog turns into man		
man pays the old woman		
	husband is accused of having mistress (promiscuous)	wife accused of going to find new husband

Given Zinacanteco criteria for human behavior, *hʔikʼal*'s would definitely be classified as bestial. He is a cannibal, promiscuous, blasphemous. He resembles a buzzard and a cat. He is asked by San

Lorenzo: "Are you a weasel that you drink my children's things? [their chicken eggs]" *H'ik'al* has wings and perhaps an animal prototype in the bat. He has multiple young and his children are born in three days, a remarkable gestation period, even for a small animal. As something that is more like an animal than not, how is *h'ik'al* to be dealt with?

In the Maya area that this discussion encompasses, there seem to be two methods of dealing with spooks: one can civilize them or destroy them. Often, these two approaches are synonymous. One throws some special concoction on them, burns them, or beats them. A man frequently molested by Black-man is advised by his brother-in-law to put tobacco at the door (RLM, tale 127). There is scarcely a spook that does not succumb to some one, or to a concoction of several, of the following ingredients: salt, garlic, tobacco, chile, or dried chile, ashes, white lime, liquor, or boiling water. All these ingredients are unique to man. Often they are used in cooking. Lime is used to soak corn, ashes are a product of the hearth. A meal in Zinacantan is not complete without salt or, on ritual occasions, a bottle of *poš*[1] on the table; a little salt may be sprinkled on the food before eating it, "to keep the demons out." Though not actually used in cooking, garlic is an important element in curing the sick. Liquor and tobacco are not exceptions, for they too are aspects of civilized living. They can be regarded as products of human processing, for they are "cooked": tobacco is burned before it is inhaled, liquor fermented before it is drunk. Like salt and liquor, smoking is an important concomitant of social ceremony. Cigarettes are not necessarily smoked by one person; instead the lighted cigarette may be passed around and shared by all the men in a group.

H'ik'al can be kept away by tobacco. He is also susceptible to being scalded and being burned in fires. Sometimes he is actually cut to pieces or skewered and roasted. Cooking again plays an important role. A third strategy used by Zinacantecos is one that I have not heard of anywhere else: they save up intestinal gas all through the night until dawn, as protection in case *h'ik'al* should come (see RML, tale 23). Two things are noteworthy about this practice.

---

[1] *Poš* is cane liquor.

Farts, like liquor or cigarette smoke, might be considered "cooked" by human processes. In another sense, however, they are the opposite of cooked food—a form of "rotten" non-food. As such, farts fit into a category of ambiguous, or "marginal," substances—neither part of the body nor unrelated to it, neither food nor never-food, and so on—and thus are part of the whole complex of anomalies that has been described for the spooks. In Highland Guatemala two spooks, *siguanaba* and *siguamonta*, are said to go about smelling the wind broken by drunkards.

The logic behind the use of ingredients like tobacco, salt, and boiling water in these tales is based on the opposition between civilized and uncivilized. Certainly, salt is part of the humanizing process of many Maya, including Zinacantecos. Salt and chile (applied to the lips) are "given" to the children at birth. Salt is applied again at baptism, and this practice is thought to seal in the *č'ulel*—or "soul"—(Jane Collier 1962–1963:Field Interview-6-1). Before baptism, the baby is thought of as something not quite human; at baptism, along with the salt, he receives a name and is incorporated into the human social order. At death, special ingredients again serve as "sealers." Instead of keeping something (the soul) in, they are keeping something (the dead) out. In San Pedro Chenalhó, "even when the death has taken place at a distance, in another house [the Pedranos] are afraid. The ground leaves of the wild tobacco are rubbed on the back of the neck, on the forehead and on the inside of the elbow and knee joints. It is this way that the dead do not come to seize us" (Guiteras-Holmes 1961:264).

People being baptized and people who survive a dead person are in transition between one realm (the human world) and another (the non-human). Likewise, a sick person is in an ambiguous position between being dead and being alive. In San Pedro Chenalhó, "when someone is ill and a *compañero* dies in the same house . . . *pilico* [the same as *moy* "wild tobacco"] is rubbed on all his joints, on his stomach, his head, and the little gourd bottle is placed at the head of the bed. In that way, *Tentación* [the devil] is frightened away . . . the *pilico* is mixed with garlic" (Guiteras-Holmes 1961: 217). Travelers are also people in transition, between one place and another. In Highland Guatemala, men who must be out on the mountain often tie dried chile to their rifles. Interestingly, in ancient Mexico, the Aztecs also used these concoctions at times of transition. A *tecomatillo* (small gourd) of *piciete* (tobacco) was worn around the neck as "strength for the road." At his royal investiture, Moctezuma fastened such a gourd around his neck (quoted from Fernando de Alvarado Tezozomoc, *Crónica Mexicana* in the *Popol Vuh* 1950:209 n. 5).

In the case of spooks, the concoction—whatever it is—acts to seal the transform off from its human identity. The witch whose husband has put salt on her skin cannot put it back on again.[2] She is forced to remain in her non-human form, and she dies. In the "Sorcery Story" from Belize, a woman takes off her head and becomes a mule. While she is gone, ashes are rubbed on her severed neck. Unable to reattach her human head, she must remain an animal. In an attempt to return to human form, her head attaches to her husband and stays there until the husband is able to lose both mule and head in the woods.

A Sorcery Story

A man had a wife who was a sorceress and used to turn herself into a mule. Every Friday she would sit up late spinning cotton, and she used to put a fire under her husband's hammock so that he wouldn't wake up with the cold. The man suspected his wife, so one Friday he kept awake. At midnight his wife put away the cotton she was spinning, and, throwing herself on the ground, after first having taken off her head and placed it on the ground, she turned into a mule; then she went off with a number of other mules.[3] The man took some ashes and rubbed them on the severed neck of her head. Just before dawn the mules returned. The woman threw herself onto the ground and changed back into human shape, but she could not fix her head on again because of the ashes. Accordingly she changed back into a mule again and, carrying the head, she followed the man wherever he went. He tried to shake her off, but

[2] In Yucatán, the reason given for a witch's removing her skin in the first place is "baptism," a belief that has interesting ramifications if, as in Zinacantán, salt is used at baptism.

[3] This story is similar to a West African one where Fari She-ass, the wife of the king, goes off with her ladies-in-waiting each evening to become mules. By trickery, her mule form is made permanent.

could not. One day he went into a very thick part of the forest and there succeeded in losing the mule and her head. The mule and head turned into an owl (*buh*). That is why the owl hoots, cries, and laughs like a woman. (Thompson 1930:158)

In these tales, a person's head attaching to an animal is analogous to that person *becoming* an animal. In the following tale from Zinacantan about the Charcoal-cruncher a series of events similar to that in the Thompson sorcery story takes place; in the Zinacanteco tale, the woman's head attaches first to her husband, then to an animal in the forest. In both cases, the concoction that was applied served a segregative function, and the spook was successfully sealed out of its human identity.

THE CHARCOAL-CRUNCHER

There was a man sleeping with his wife. You see she was a charcoal-cruncher.

Well, the man touched his wife in the dark. She wasn't there, just a part of her was there. She had no head.

You see he looked at her. He lit the fire. "Where did my wife go?" he said. "Why did this happen? Where did her head go? How could someone have cut her head off?" said her husband. "Oh, who knows? Maybe there's some reason. Maybe she's evil. Maybe [her head] went for a walk," said her husband. "No, let's see what this does to her if she is a devil." He put salt where the severed part was. He put salt on it.

Well, when [her head] arrived it couldn't hold fast. So her head just rolled around like a [sacrificed] chicken. It just bounced and bounced now. "Why are you doing this to me? Why are you doing this?" the woman asked her husband when she arrived.

"But why do you go take a walk, then? Are you a devil? It's because you're a devil!" he told his wife.

Now she cried, "Well, but how can it be? But where can I go now that my flesh doesn't mend?" said the woman.

"Oh, I don't know. See for yourself. I don't want to be with you anymore. What you're doing is too awful," her husband replied.

You see, it bounced and landed on his shoulder. That's where it landed. He had two heads now. The man had two heads. "Ah, but this is no good," he said. He prayed to Our Lord. "My Lord, but why is this? This is awful. If the other one holds fast I'll have two faces," said the man. "One, a woman's, the other, a man's. This is terrible," he said. What can

I do about it? What?" he said. "What if Our Lord doesn't help me? If only there were something, if there were something, if there were someone who would take it away. Have him go, have him go and get rid of it," he said.

He tricked her. "Well, it's nothing. Come down a minute! Stay there on the ground! I'm going to climb the pine tree. I'm going to bring down some pine kernels for you to eat, for us to eat. "Will you eat them?" he asked his wife.

"Go on then! Climb up then." He climbed up the pine tree.

Well, when he climbed the tree, the woman's head bounced and bounced at the foot of the pine. It bounced but it didn't land high enough. It was going to climb the tree. "God, My Lord, but what can I do about this. Isn't there something. If there were something. If there were something to come and take it away for me," said the man. "Well, eat, please!" he told her. He dropped the pine kernels down.

Well, a deer came along.

Well (the woman's head) landed and stuck to the deer's back. The deer was terribly frightened by it. To this day deer are very wild. It was scared. It rushed off. That's how the woman's head was lost. That's how the story ends. (RML, tale 60)

Isolated from its human identity, the charcoal-cruncher either becomes an animal or (as in RML, tales 47 and 81) it dies. In tale 81, the wife of a male charcoal-cruncher puts salt on his severed neck. The head returns and bounces around helplessly. It lands on his child, but his head "didn't stick on"; eventually the charcoal-cruncher starves to death. In both myths, the death of the spook is clearly established by burying it in a cemetery grave. Structurally then, permanently becoming an animal is equivalent to being killed. In both cases, a definite boundary between the human world and the spook's realm is established.

The concoction acts as a stabilizer; it divests the spook of ambiguity. For instance, the identity of Skeleton-woman (RML, tale 73) is highly ambiguous. She is a living woman with a husband and children that nurse, but, in addition, she is a creature that starves herself, that is shrunken with an ugly face, a wife who does not talk or argue. In short, she is a corpse-eater that removes her flesh to go about as a skeleton. Traveling each night between her home and the cemetery, she is a creature that mediates between the living and the dead. In behavior and aspect, she already resembles the dead. When her husband puts salt on her flesh, and she cannot put her flesh back on, she becomes a skeleton permanently. She dies and is buried in a cemetery. Finally, her allegiance is disambiguated: she completely belongs to the world of the dead.

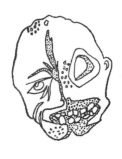

Split-faced man is a Zinacanteco spook whose face is half-black, half-white. My guess is that the dark side of his face represents flesh, the white half, bone,[4] something on the order of the ancient life-death masks found at pre-classic Tlatilco. (One of Laughlin's informants suggests that Split-faced man is the Pope.) "Twice he was killed, but he did not die. The third time he died, they gave him tobacco, they gave him garlic, salt, everything" (VRB, 106). He is half-alive, half-dead. Not until he has been saturated with "civilizing" substances is he completely dead and sealed out from one side of his ambiguous identity.

Thus, one way to rid oneself of an anomalous creature is to "civilize" or to "humanize" it, by cooking it or by applying culinary ingredients like salt, lime, or ashes. If the ambiguity in its identity is between nature and culture, life and death, these treatments work as sealers or disambiguating substances. Since he belongs to the same set of anomalous creatures, it seems natural that the civilizing ingredients should be effective against *h'ik'al* as well. The reason these ingredients are not cited *more* often in the myths may be because, though *h'ik'al* is certainly anomalous, he is permanently inhuman. Since he does not change shape, he has no alternative identity into which he might be sealed. When they do occur (see RML, tale 127 for tobacco, tale 23 for farts) it is because themes of anomaly in one ambiguous situation carry over into another. Most frequently, *h'ik'al* is simply killed by scalding or by roasting[5] —civilizing deaths akin to being cooked.

[4] *Skeleton-woman*
　　living:dead::flesh:skeleton::home:cemetery
　Split-faced man
　　living:dead::flesh:skeleton::black:white

[5] I am not at all sure about the distinction made here between those spooks with alternate identities and those without. The buzzard-man for example is a man who turns into a bird (who has two identities) but, like Black-man, is always destroyed by fire. It is true however that his is a permanent change, and Buzzard-man does not try to return to his human form.

Table 13. *Index of Civilizing Ingredients*

Ingredient	Type of Protection Obtained	Method
Salt–Garlic–Tobacco		
Zinacantan (RML)	against Charcoal-cruncher	apply to severed head
Zinacantan (VRB)	against Split-faced man	
Salt and Tobacco (Pilico)		
San Pedro Chenalhó (Guiteras-Holmes)	for a sick person	rub on all joints, and on stomach; place bottle at foot of bed
San Juan Chamelco	against *duendes*	
Tobacco		
Aztecs (Fernando de Alvarado Tezozomoc)	"strength for the road"	in *tecomatilla* (small gourd) around neck
Lime ("Cal")		
Panajachel (Tax)	against *cbaracotel*	place at door
Zinacantan (RML)	against *b'ik'al*	rub on neck, forehead, and inside of elbow
San Pedro Chenalhó (Guiteras-Holmes)	put on the dead so that they don't seize anyone else	
Tobacco, Garlic, Foxroot, or Liquor		
San Pedro Chenalhó (Guiteras-Holmes)	cures snakebite, dogbite, sorcery	
Coals, Garlic, Meal		
Europe (Leland)		hang about a child's neck
Palo de Chichicaste		
Panajachel (Tax)	against *cbaracotel* or Carnero-woman	
San Pedro La Laguna (Paul)	against *cbaracotel*	

(Continued on next page)

Ingredient	Type of Protection Obtained	Method
Fart		
Zinacantan (RML)	against *bʔikʼal*	
Chile		
Samayac (Blaffer)	against night spirts	burn it in fire
Santo Tomás Chichicastenango (Tax)	for travelers on the mountain	hang from rifle
Boiling Water		
Zinacantan (RML)	against *bʔikʼal*;	
	keeps *pukuhetik* out	
Salt		
Zinacantan (RML)	against *charcoal-cruncher*	sprinkle on food before eating
	against corpse-eater	apply to neck
	against *yalen beket*	apply to discarded flesh
		apply to flesh left at cross
San Pedro Chenalhó (Guiteras-Holmes)	against witch	apply to discarded skin
Yucatán (Castillo)	against *characotel*	apply to skin left at cross
Panajachel (Tax)	against witch	apply to flesh or discarded skin
Southern U.S. (see rubric, ch. 5)	salt is avoided by parents of	
Africa-Ndembu (Turner)	novices who are being initiated	
Garlic		
Zinacantan (Zabala)	white bundle (a spook)	
	throws garlic onto sick people	

Demons and animals with short and long hair become tame from being talked to (Asturias 1967).

2. Domesticating a Spook

Another way to deal with spooks is to tame
them. The theme of domestication is already implicit in the identity
of some spooks. The distinguishing feature of the *characotel* from
northwestern Guatemala is the chain hanging from the spook's neck.
A story is told in San Pedro la Laguna about a man emerging from a
cantina who was butted by a burro. At first people thought the
animal had just got loose, but then they saw it had a chain around
its neck—"Therefore it was a *characotel*" (Paul 1962:3859–3860).
A *characotel* always transforms itself into a domestic animal, usually
into a dog or a goat. This werewolf, or "carnero-woman," may also
wear a bit of rope or corn cob about its neck; the leader of a group
of *characoteles* may wear a bell. The way to master a *characotel* is to
catch hold of the chain and then beat the creature with whips of
chichicaste as it flies through the air.[6]

The fact that the animal is a domestic one and that it wears something about its neck suggests a runaway creature—analogous to the
human wife gone wild that changes into a *characotel*. This opposition between animal-man, wild-tame is emphasized again by the
use of *chichicaste* whips. *Chichicaste*, or nettle tree (*Utera bacci-
fera*), is the universal hedge plant in northwestern Guatemala from
which the town Chichicastenango derives its name (McBryde
1945:148). A hedge or a fence is the concrete manifestation of a
conceptual separation between the human world and the animal
world.

Some of the prime entertainment at San Sebastian involves
h?ik'aletik and *bolometik* beating their stuffed animals with *chicote*
whips.[7] These whips have no special connotations that I know of
but, since they are used under similar circumstances elsewhere, they
may be part of a general scheme for dealing with deviant or

---

[6] In Panajachel, salt is thrown on the *characotel* as well (Tax 1950).

[7] The word *chicote* is used in America to mean whip. In Spain it refers to a
cigar stub. In nautical usage *chicotes* are ropes or the end of ropes.

anomalous behavior. For example, in Chichicastenango little spirit men known as *encantos* beat their victims with *chicotes* (Tax 1947: 469); these same *encantos* have a reputation for whipping unfaithful spouses. At San Sebastian the stuffed squirrels and monkeys who are punished with sticks represent women who have gotten out of hand. They are oversexed wives who have led their office-holding husbands astray. Like the *hʔik'aletik* who punish them, they behave like promiscuous animals. As deviants who disregard human norms, both sets of malefactors must be dealt with. Near the finale of San Sebastian, the house of the *bolometik*—which is also considered the home of *hʔik'aletik* (Vogt 1960; Interview with Domingo de la Torre Perez)—is burned. The two *bolometik* are killed and then revived—their souls "exchanged" for those of two Chamula boys who, as was pointed out in chapter 2 are human but also alien. At *karnaval, tot hʔik'al* and his *hʔik'aletik* are temporarily jailed and then released. Is it possible that these beatings and imprisonments, the killing and revival through human agents, are not meant simply as punishment, but rather as forms of taming and rehabilitation, analogous to the treatment of *characoteles* who are caught by their chains and beaten with *chichicaste*?

> *Siguanaba*, the warrior woman of solitary canyons and *Siguamonta* the warrior woman of canyons that are near populated forests, villages or cities . . . were on the lookout for drunkards who were apt to forget quite quickly that they were bipeds and start to walk like quadrupeds. (Asturias 1967)

3. Drunks, Idiots, and Sleepers

As was suggested in the introduction, there is a set of anomalies involving ambiguous creatures, conditions, and habits. A corollary of this is that people in anomalous conditions are most susceptible to anomalous creatures. Throughout the Maya area, wherever he appears, Black-man's victims are nearly always drunk, asleep, or crazy.[8]

[8] The point that drunks, dreamers, and hallucinators are those people most likely to encounter spectres—just as they might "pink elephants"—may well be true, but I don't think this observation is incompatible wtih the structural explanation.

The oppositions animal-man, dead-alive, male-female (discussed in the next section) are relevant not only to the spooks, but apply also to their victims; people in a hard-to-classify situation are fair game for spooks. People somewhere between these poles are most susceptible. The *chamen winik* of Cancuc (Guiteras-Holmes 1946: 139) and the *characotel* and *cadejo* of Highland Guatemala pay specific attention to drunks. In Zinacantan, a demon called *špak'in teʔ* (Laughlin 1963 Fieldnotes) performs something on the order of a "breatherizer" test; she stops drunks and makes them urinate (Laughlin 1963 Fieldnotes). Likewise, the *siguanaba* (Asturias 1967) recognizes drunkards by the wind they break. The Chorti Maya (Wisdom 1940) believe that a meeting with the *siguanaba* renders the victim insane. Drunks and idiots share a state that is between total consciousness and death.

According to Tzotzil beliefs, the soul departs from the body during such times of semiconsciousness. Each man has two souls, an inner personal soul, the *č'ulel* (sometimes spelled *ch'ulel*), located in the heart of each person, and an animal soul, the *čanul* (also *chanul*). The *č'ulel* is also found in the blood that is connected to the heart and is thought to have thirteen parts, any one of which may be lost. The Tzotzil speakers of San Pedro Chenalhó believe that it is this *č'ulel* that departs from the body during sleep, unconsciousness, apparent death, and coitus (Guiteras-Holmes 1961: 297). This belief also exists in Zinacantan where any frightening situation—for instance, falling down or seeing a demon (*pukuh*) on a dark night—is cause for *šiʔel* (sometimes spelled *shi'el*), or "soul-loss" (Vogt 1968:15). In Zinacantan, there is a close relation between the *č'ulel*, the *čanul*, and social control. Deviant behavior, which includes breaking the moral code or flouting values central to Zinacanteco culture, can lead to *šiʔel* (Vogt 1969:37).[9]

A person with only part of a soul is in a highly vulnerable position. In San Pedro Chenalhó, it is said that "when the *ch'ulel* [*č'ulel*] leaves, the body becomes as meat to be eaten" (Guiteras-Holmes 1961:220). Complete soul-loss results in death, its total presence means well-being. The *hʔik'al* myths are fairly explicit on

[9] In Agua Escondida and among the Chorti a person who is immoral or "of little faith" is particularly vulnerable to spooks.

the relationship between soul-loss and vulnerability. A drunken traveler (RML, tale 127) regains partial consciousness when Black-man pours water over his face; a literal translation reads, "the man's soul entered a little." In all but one (RML, tale 124) of the tales where *hʔikʼal* accosts travelers, his victims are asleep on the road. In three of the four stories about *hʔikʼal*'s molesting women, his victims are asleep by the fire. In an obscure version from Oxchuc, insanity is blamed on being kidnapped by *hʔikʼal*, though it could also be that *hʔikʼal prefers* insane or retarded victims.

The condition of ambiguity accompanying soul-loss may explain the *karnaval* injunction against *hʔikʼaletik* falling asleep. In particular, it is feared that if a *tot hʔikʼal* went to sleep he would die. Bricker records the case of a man who had served several years as *hʔikʼal* without mishap. On one particular occasion, however, he was overcome with fatigue and fell asleep. Sure enough, he grew ill and decided to discontinue his role as *tot hʔikʼal*. Since *hʔikʼal* is a spook closely associated with death, a man impersonating him is treading on dangerous ground. He needs every bit of protection; should his soul go off in sleep, the impersonator of *hʔikʼal* might fall victim to his own suggestion.

A curious practice in San Pedro Chenalhó underscores the increased hazards of soul-loss during ritual performances. Guiteras-Holmes asked her informant why those couples who have had intercourse have to be ritually "revived" during *karnaval*. Her informant Manuel explained that this is the case only in *special* instances. "With the sexual act, man's and woman's *chʼulel* [*čʼulel*] leave the body, but in everyday life it does not have to be called back as one does for *komel* [or *espanto*]:[10] the *chʼulel* [*čʼulel*] escapes a little but returns" (1961:222).

Before closing this discussion of anomalous conditions, I should also mention the case of blindness. The victim lives in a state of visual darkness resembling sleep or death. In San Pedro la Laguna, a *characotel* who steals the bell from the church of San Juan grows blind and dies (Paul 1962:3877). Bricker records a myth in which

---

[10] This is not the term *espanto* as I use it to designate "spook." Guiteras-Holmes uses it to mean illness caused by shock or sudden fright, entailing soul-loss—what Zinacantecos call *šiʔel*.

a Black-man warns that anyone who enters his cave will go blind. The "little old lady" (tale 130) that *hʔikʼal* carries off *is* blind, and it may be that *hʔikʼal* himself is sometimes blind. In tale 130 Black-man has been pestering the Holy Martyr continuously, asking for children. The Holy Martyr promises twice to give him someone, but both times *hʔikʼal* is tricked. *Hʔikʼal* mistakes first a horse and then a thornbush for a person. He is told, "It's because you can't see well, you're blind."[11]

[11] This blindness could possibly have to do with the bat prototype; I favor the structural explanation.

vi. Hʔik'al as a Clarifying Anomaly

The most dangerous dwarf I've ever known . . . She
does the same thing to all women. She lies in wait for
them on the streets in the dark and snatches away their
sex (Asturias 1967).

1. Conditions That Are Ambiguous

Women in Zinacantan are considered danger-
ous;[1] as Laughlin puts it, female sexuality must be "handled deli-
cately" (Laughlin 1963:99). For instance, only ancient women
(who are like neuter persons) may fill the formal religious posts
open to their sex. In both Zinacantan and San Pedro Chenalhó, a
woman must never step over a man, because she has more "heat"
(Guiteras-Holmes 1961:119, and personal communication from
Jane Collier). Women in certain conditions are particularly danger-

Auitzotl, a
spectral
water animal
who eats the
nails and
hair of
drunkards

[1] Though psychological explanations have been suggested, I do not feel quali-
fied to offer an opinion. It is true though that anxiety on the subject of women is
frequently evidenced in Zinacanteco and Chamula folktales.

ous.[2] Zinacantecos believe that pregnant women cause soul-loss. If such women come near meat freshly slaughtered by their husbands, they will cause it to putrefy (Laughlin 1963:99). Similarily, during the Chamula celebration of *karnaval* pregnant women and all men (in case their wives or mistresses are pregnant) bite the breast of a sacrificed bull to ensure that the meat won't putrefy. Zinacanteco men believe that if they have intercourse with a woman during her period that her "sickness," as they call it, will cause them to have cramps as well (Laughlin 1963:99). In San Pedro Chenalhó, a menstruating woman does not approach the place where quicklime is being burnt, in order not to spoil the men's work by "blackening" the stones and making them exude a bloodlike substance.[3]

Women in the Maya area have a grave responsibility to watch over their sexuality in order to safeguard the well-being of those around them. In particular, women who are in ambiguous conditions—a pregnant woman,[4] who is neither one person nor two, or a menstruating woman (to be discussed later), who exudes waste—must be careful. Furthermore, these conditions are equivalent to other anomalous states; for example in Yucatán, at Chan Kom, a menstruating woman and a corpse are equally dangerous to a man with a wound (Redfield and Villa Rojas 1934). Similarly, beliefs surrounding unusual circumstances of birth demonstrate a conceptual tie between such special conditions and other anomalies. In San Pedro la Laguna and Santa Lucia Uxtatlán, a person born with a veil is thought to be a *characotel*; in Zinacantan, if a foetus is born dead, its soul becomes a *špak'in te?* (Laughlin 1963 Fieldnotes).[5]

---

[2] Douglas (1968:95) describes such people as "somehow left out of the patterning of society, who are placeless. Even if they have done nothing morally wrong, their status is undefinable."

[3] This association of blood with blackening may be reflected in the Zinacanteco term for *'ik'al*, which designates the drops of blood made when the midwife cuts into the umbilical cord of a newborn (Ancheutz 1966a Fieldnotes).

[4] In Zinacantan, pregnancy and childbirth are classified as *čamel* "body sickness" (Ancheutz 1966b:1).

[5] Even in the case of normal births, something interesting may be going on with the developing baby. In San Pedro Chenalhó, a foetus is said to start out as a mouse. A month later it becomes a toad. Not until the third month does

A woman who is careless with her sexuality is no different from a cargo official intemperate in office (see chapter 2, part 2); both exhibit the kind of anomalous behavior that may cause soul-loss in other people. Both involve a failure to properly fulfill sex-allocated roles: the woman heedful of her sexuality, the man responsible in political office. Both are anomalous because they deviate from the behavior expected of them and would thus be fair game for spooks who are anomalous creatures (who in turn search out victims who are likewise in ambiguous conditions; see also chapter 5, part 3). At San Sebastian, Zinacantecos are punished by *ħʔik'aletik* for behavior that does not coincide with the ideal norm for their sex. While negligent cargoholders are ridiculed for weakness, their wives are publicly accused of being oversexed.[6] In Zinacantan, a man who succumbs to sexual temptation at a time when he should abstain is a weak man, or he has an oversexed wife—something no man wants, because it challenges his own masculinity and leaves him vulnerable to cuckoldry (Bricker 1968:279). Likewise, a man presiding in office who cannot exercise moderation in drink is considered soft.

In the myths, too, *ħʔik'al* attacks both sexes, but he is rarely successful against males, at least not against the brave ones. The issue of bravery versus cowardice is often discussed in those tales where *ħʔik'al* accosts men-travelers asleep on the road (see charts for RML, tales 123, 124, 125, 126, 127 and EZV F-I8). Frequently, one of the men is described as frightened, the other as "strong of heart." The brave mans asks his companion: "What are you scared of? What the hell, are you blue-assed?" (The translator's note here reads: "Do you wear women's skirts?" [RML, tale 123]) In another tale he asks his companion: "Hell, aren't you a man? Haven't you any balls?" (RML, tale 126) His question implies that a man who is not brave is also not a man; the courageous man is scornful and treats his companion like a woman: "I am a brave man. Put a lot of

---

it resemble a human infant (Guiteras-Holmes 1961:103), and I wonder if these foetuses might not be considered analogous to transforming animals.

   6 Though I am only discussing here the part played by *ħʔik'aletik*, it is important to remember that *bolometik* participate as well in this mocking.

firewood on [if your ass is frightened blue]" (RML, tale 123).
Elsewhere the strong man asks his friend before starting out whether
he is brave and is assured by his friend that he is. When the two
are accosted by *hʔik'al*, however, the friend exhibits cowardice and
is reprimanded by the braver man: "You didn't tell the truth—that
you are brave" (RML, tale 26). After the rescue of the Magdalenas
girl, one man marries her and the other gets "a good beating." "I
thought I was brave. I wasn't brave at all" (RML, tale 123). The
man who is afraid (but who claims that he is brave) grows cold and
shivers with fright, or else he urinates on himself. His brave companion, on the other hand, stands up to *hʔik'al*, and shoots or stabs
him. In all these tales of Black-man accosting travelers, the man
who defeats *hʔik'al* takes the wings from his feet and flies off to
Black-man land; he gets Black-man's money, marries the girl rescued from him, or is given a meal by her father. In other words, the
man who acts as a man should, who is virile and unafraid, is rewarded. In the one instance (RML, tale 127) where neither of the
two travelers defeats *hʔik'al* and neither receives a reward, both men
are helplessly drunk when *hʔik'al* arrives and neither one distin-
guishes himself. *Hʔik'al* has to wake up his victim by dousing him
with cold water. The man runs away to his house and is thereafter
plagued repeatedly by *hʔik'al* until he is advised to put tobacco at
his door.

Again, in the tales where Black-man asks for children (RML,
tales 68 and 130) there is a hint that people who behave well need
not fear the *hʔik'al*. Black-man asks the Holy Martyr for "company"
and is told: "Me, I'll never give away my children . . . I'm content
with my children. They remember to bring me my flowers. They
remember to bring me my candles, at dusk and at dawn" Later in
the same tale the saint repeats: "But me, I'm satisfied that they
sweep my house . . . they always come to give me flowers . . . candles
. . . incense. It's true not all of them do that . . . But whoever it is
they each take turns" (RML, tale 130).

In these tales the saints protect their children (who are faithful)
from *hʔik'al*. In the tales where *hʔik'al* accosts travelers, it is only
the cowardly or pseudo-brave man who is most likely to suffer;

TABLE 14. Stories about Hʔik'al Molesting Women

RML, *tales*	23	67	71	122
All begin with some invocation to the effect that there were many Blackmen			just women	Men are gone
			the woman is asleep at edge of fire	
She	is	cooking	corn	or *atole*
nixtamal boils over		woman seized pouring out *nixtamal*		
The murdered	woman's	blood	hisses	on the fire
(This	is	the	sound	*pululu*)
Her comadre calls that corn must be ready				
	formerly people withheld farts to protect themselves	the women gather to defend themselves	they put poles at edge of fire to protect the woman	
		women pour boiling water on *hʔik'al*, then burn him in fire	they shoot *hʔik'al*, scald him, burn his baby, cut his flesh to pieces	
			hunters rescue woman from *hʔik'al*'s cave	
			Black-man's children are lined up on the edge of her skirt	
			they burn *hʔik'al*'s children	
			rescued woman dies urinating lime water	

Table 15. Stories about Hʔikʼal Accosting Travelers

RML, tale 127	FI-8	RWL, tales 123[1]	I24	I26	I25
On the way home from Chamula a man meets his brother-in-law.	one or two men are asleep on *cerro*	two men asleep in a cave		two travelers asleep by path	traveler is asleep half-way up mountain
Together they get drunk.		one man is scared		they are cold; one is frightened and beset by chills	man is frightened
Though he is drunk, the man decides to try to make it home; his wife might not lock up properly.	traveler awakes to see *bʔikʼal*	man urinates on himself	Chamula meets Black-man on path		
But as he tries to jump over the stream, he stumbles and falls asleep right there.	traveler is eating beans by the fire	comes to warm himself by fire		crouched by fire	Black-man is crouched by the fire
"His soul didn't enter" again (he didn't wake up) until he felt the Black-man carrying him off.		men and spook smoke together	they fight		
Hʔikʼal proceeds to wash the man's face, pouring water over it, because he thinks it is burning.		they fight with swords			
The drunk rushes away to his house, is followed by the Black-man.	man shoots *bʔikʼal*	Black-man is stabbed to death; also hanged	Chamula wins the fight	the fearful man of the two shoots *bʔikʼal*; the other kills him	man shoots Black-man and cuts him to pieces
Hʔikʼal enters the house and attacks the chickens; the next morning half of them are wounded.		Black-man dies urinating "his filth"			
The second night, *bʔikʼal* attacks their pig. The next morning there is a puddle of blood; the dog's ear has been sliced off.	man finds something behind *bʔikʼal's* feet and puts them on		he pulls off *bʔikʼal's* wings and puts them on himself		puts Black-man's wings on himself

[1] Issues of cowardice, bravery, and manliness figure in the discussions of the travelers.

Table 15, continued

RML, tale 127	FI-8	RWL, tales 123[1]	124	126	125
Hʔikʹal comes a third night, looking for chickens, and drinks up their eggs.	he flies to pueblo of bʔikʹal and returns		he flies to Black-man's home and returns		he visits Black-man's home
Some months later, bʔikʹal resumes his attacks; the son of that man and his wife complain of feeling a freezing cold hand upon his shoulder.		they find a girl from Magdalena wrapped up in straw mat		they find girl from San Andrés wrapped in a straw mat	
The mother searches for bʔikʹal, but cannot see him because he looks so much like a cat.	bʔikʹal gives them money before they kill him	man marries rescued girl	man hopes to get bʔikʹal's buried money	they return girl to her home and are rewarded	the Black-man gives him money
The man shoots at bʔikʹal and, somehow, Black-man gets impaled on a pole.					
When the man's brother-in-law comes to visit, all of these problems with the bʔikʹal are repeated for him; he suggests putting holy water and tobacco at the door to guard it.					

[1] Issues of cowardice, bravery, and manliness figure in the discussions of the travelers.

Table 16. The Black-man Asks for Children

RML, tale 130	*RML, tale 68*
Hʔikʼal goes to the Holy Martyr to ask for children, who refuses because he is pleased with them.	
Hʔikʼal then asks San Lorenzo, who likewise refuses; his children bring him candles and flowers and clean his house.	*Hʔikʼal asks* San Lorenzo for children. When "Lol" won't give him any, he asks San Juan, or "Shun."
Exasperated by *hʔikʼal*'s persistence, "Larry" tricks him, telling *hʔikʼal* that he will give him the person (really a mule) coming along the road.	
Hʔikʼal complains about getting kicked and is told: it's "because you're blind."	
Again, *hʔikʼal* is tricked, this time into thinking a hawthorn tree is a person; he is hurt by thorns that prick his face.	
The third time *hʔikʼal* is tricked, he falls off a bridge into the river.	
At this point "Larry" rails at Black-man for stealing his children's chickens and eggs.	
Finally the saint "Johnny" (San Juan) does give him someone: a little old lady who is blind and who "wasn't good for anything."	San Juan agrees to give him some, and apparently that's why Chamulas die from assassins.
Hʔikʼal carried her off but frightened her so badly that she dies.	
Next *hʔikʼal* attacks a boy riding a horse; the boy is thrown and *hʔikʼal* carries him off to his cave.	
Hʔikʼal captures a second person, this time a young girl who is kneading clay by the door.	
She mistakes Black-man for a buzzard and is taken to his cave to prepare food for him.	
On the third night after her arrival, she bears him a baby Black-man; it grows up in one night.	
The girl's uncle rescues her from the deep cave with a lasso.	
But the rescue is too late, since she is already beginning to swell. It is terribly cold, she has been sunk in the water (?) "as if dead." The swelling is also attributed to Black-man's long penis.	
She arrives home to die.	

Table 17. The "Tacked-on" Tales

A. *RML, tales 123*	*126*
two travelers defeat and kill Black-man	the braver of two travelers kills Black-man
They find a girl from Magdalena wrapped in a straw mat	they find a girl from San Andrés wrapped in a straw mat
	she was seized while pouring out her *nixtamal*
the braver man marries her	the men bring her home and are rewarded by a meal
one of the men, although it is not really clear which one, is beaten with a switch	

B. *RML, tales 71*	*130*
a girl is carried off by *hʔikʼal* while pouring out her *nixtamal*	a girl sitting by the door kneading clay is carried off by *hʔikʼal*
	she thinks Black-man is a buzzard
	she does the cooking for Black-man
	the night after her arrival, she bears a baby Black-man that grows up in one day
hunters rescue her from the deep cave with a lasso	her uncle rescues her from the deep cave with a lasso
hʔikʼal's children are lined up on the edge of her skirt	her children are lined up on the edge of her skirt
they burn *hʔikʼal*'s child in the fire	she throws her offspring back into the cave
the girl is not home a month when she dies, urinating lime water	after several months at home, the girl swells up and dies (from *hʔikʼal*'s long penis and from being sunk in water)
hʔikʼal continues to search for his "wife"	
he is shot, scalded, and cut into pieces	

brave men seem to be rewarded.[7] In the tales where *h?ik'al* molests women, however, no one is rewarded. Instead the victim is raped and murdered, or else carried away to Black-man's cave. Given the moralistic overtones of these myths, we might suspect that there has been some sin of omission or some failure to fulfill culturally defined roles—the sort of departure from norms that qualifies someone as "not a proper woman," or anomalous.

> A young man had arranged to meet his sweetheart in the forest on the edge of the village. When he arrived at the tryst, he saw what he thought was his sweetheart, but it was a *xtabai* in her form. He advanced to meet her but the *xtabai* walked backwards so as not to show her hollow back, which was like the rough bark of a tree. The youth at last overtook her and putting his arms around her embraced her. He felt her back to be hollow and realized it was not the girl but *xtabai*. He began to pray whereupon the *xtabai* turned into a heap of rotten wood. The man made a fire and burned the rotten wood, and in this way destroyed the *xtabai*. The girl whom he had gone to visit and whom the *xtabai* had impersonated took sick at the same moment, and three days later died.
>
> (Thompson 1930:157)

2. Hard or Careless Women and Soft Men

One of the consistent patterns in these tales of rape or murder is that the woman is seized while throwing out her *nixtamal* (lime water) (RML, tales 71, 126) or while asleep by the fire cooking corn (RML, tales 23, 67, 71, and 122), and the sound *pululu huštale* is made by her blood hissing on the fire.

---

[7] The characterizations ("brave" versus "cowardly") in these tales are by no means clear. The man who claims to be "brave" may behave like a coward; the man who admits to his fears, who is cautious, may be the one who best copes with the situation. I am grateful to Gary Crocker for pointing out this possible source of confusion.

Whenever the corn or *atole* boils over and makes this sound, it is said that *hʔikʾal* is near.

The girl is seized under the following conditions:

1. Pouring out *nixtamal* (RML, tales 126 and 71)
2. Kneading clay (RML, tale 130)
3. Cooking corn; the mixture spills over and hisses on the fire (making the sound *pululu*) (RML, tales 122, 67, 71, and 23)

In tale 71, this theme has a strange twist: there the woman dies urinating lime water.

Before going on to the theme of throwing out the *nixtamal*, I will discuss briefly how *nixtamal* is used, point out the analogies that Zinacantecos draw between making tortillas and making babies, and indulge in an excursus on waste.

This aqueous solution, called by its Aztec name *nixtamal*, is used for boiling and softening corn throughout most of Mexico and Guatemala. After treatment, the corn can easily be ground on the stone for making tortillas, tamales, and posoles, or other derivatives of the maize paste sometimes called *masa* (McBryde 1945:60). One Zinacanteco informant (Jose Perez Hernandes in a 1968 interview with E. Z. Vogt) suggests that what is actually boiling over in these Black-man tales is a special *nixtamal* without lime called *huš*, which is used for *atole* rather than for tortillas.

In Zinacantan, the term used both for making tortillas and for making babies is the same; this verb, *melṭan*, is also used to designate the making of political affairs. Interestingly, the chief social functions of each sex—cooking and childbirth for women, political affairs for men—are encompassed by this word. Such an analogy between making tortillas and making babies fits in well with the Zinacanteco conceptualization of the developing foetus. During the first months of pregnancy the foetus is said to have the consistency of *atole*.

Zinacantecos believe that at pregnancy a woman's blood stops flowing because it is diverted into forming the flesh of the foetus (Laughlin 1963 Fieldnotes). The corollary of this view qualifies menstrual blood as waste: it is the blood *not* used in making babies. If

atole	is used in making (*melȼan*)	tortillas
	and	
menstrual blood	is used in making (*melȼan*)	babies

and if the early foetus made of menstrual blood resembles *atole*, *nixtamal* (waste from *atole*) is, by extension, a fair equivalent to menstrual blood (waste from the flesh of an unmade foetus).

Various kinds of waste and what might be called "marginal substances"[8] crop up frequently in tales about anomalous creatures. Some spooks like *xtabai* in Yucatán and in Belize and *špak'in te?* in Zinacantan actually turn into excrement or rotten wood. Like the little Mexican *auitzotl* that consumes the nails and hair of drunkards, eating marginal substances is a common function of spooks. In Zinacantan, there are corpse-eater and charcoal-cruncher. The man-turned-dog eats excrement, while *h?ik'al* is notorious for cooking the blood of his victims.[9] A remark from Robert Laughlin suggests that all these waste substances are conceptually equivalent: to a Zinacanteco, a charcoal diet provokes a revulsion akin to his reaction against eating corpses. Laughlin speculates that this revulsion stems from the belief that in the afterworld the fuel of the eternal fires is provided by the bones of the dead (1963:190; also RML, tale 9). The idea of behaving like a scavenger—eating something found dead, especially something reminiscent of human dead—is disgusting. But, more important for this discussion, all these substances could be categorized as waste that is between one condition and another, as something rotten that is neither whole nor disintegrated, as excretions that are neither part of the body nor unrelated to it, neither food nor never-food, or as fuel that is neither wood nor not-wood.

Waste is one unavoidable aspect of human life, yet it is never quite assimilated into it. Though a constant by-product of culture, refuse remains always on the outskirts of civilized existence. Simi-

---

[8] Douglas says of these: "If they are pulled this way or that the shape of fundamental experience is altered. Any structure of ideas is vulnerable at its margins. We should expect the orifices of the body to symbolize its specially vulnerable points. Matter issuing from it is marginal stuff of the most obvious kind" (Douglas 1968:121). It would be a mistake, she adds, "to treat bodily margins in isolation from all other margins."

[9] Though Black-man apparently *is* a cannibal, it is never made clear in these tales whether he actually consumes this boiled blood.

larly, the evacuation of waste from the body is a necessary function
of being alive, yet its products are considered marginal. The most
obvious processes of evacuation are urination, defecation, and, for
women, menstruation. In the Zinacanteco world, food waste is immediately consumed by domestic animals. As has been mentioned,
human waste, excrement, is also eaten, usually by dogs. Ashes and
charcoal represent another kind of waste, residue left from the civilized occupation of cooking. Corn that boils over, as well as the
nixtamal used to soften it, are also examples of waste.

Tale 130 in which *hʔikʼal*'s victim sits by the door softening clay
is one of the few situations where *hʔikʼal* attacks a woman not associated with corn boiling over or with throwing out the *nixtamal*.
But, though it does not have to do with waste, softening clay, like
boiling corn in lime water, is a feminine activity. Many of a Zinacanteco woman's functions have to do with softening things and
being soft. Besides softening the corn by soaking it in *nixtamal*—a
job that a man never does—a woman prepares clay for pottery by
kneading it. Childbirth is also related to softening actions. During
labor a woman's belly is massaged with camphor ointment. If birth
is long and arduous, her belly may be rubbed with rattlesnake grease
to keep it soft (Laughlin 1963 Fieldnotes).

As with the analogy between making tortillas and making babies,
it may be that a connection is also made between preparing clay and
creating humans. Throughout the Maya area, tales are told about an
early race of men fashioned from clay. Cline records the following
from a creation myth told to him by a Lacandon living on the shore
of Lake Pelja:

When the earth was all ready he [*Hohotsakyum*, apparently the god
known elsewhere as "younger brother"—S.B.] made man. First came
the *Kalsia* [teller said he was a *kalsia*], which is to say "people of the
monkey," then came *Koho-ka*, people of the peccary, then *Ka-Puk*, or
people of the tiger [jaguar] and then *Chaoka*, or people of the pheasant.
This is how he made people. He made them out of clay, men, women,
and children, giving them eyes, ears, and all other parts, and he put the
clay on the fire where he was cooking tortillas. The clay got hard from
the fire and the people lived. After they had left he gave each people on
earth a place to live—he had to make clay babies and children so that

there would be people on earth after the first adults died (Cline 1944: 107–115).

I do not know whether the Tzotzil Maya share this belief about early men who were made from clay, but I suspect that they do or once did. At any rate, both kneading clay and throwing out the *nixtamal* involve softening processes related to female activities—making tortillas, preparing clay for pottery, and, perhaps, making babies. As such, kneading clay would be an adequate substitute in these tales for throwing out the *nixtamal*.

As I have tried to suggest, *nixtamal*, used for making tortillas, may be a metaphor for menstrual blood, the substance babies are made of. When the corn boils over and makes the sound *pululu huštale*, the narrator indicates that it is really the woman's blood hissing on the fire. Once again, blood and *atole* are confused. This equivalence is emphasized in tale 71 where the woman who is seized while throwing out her *nixtamal* dies urinating lime water—a condition that I suspect is equivalent to a menstruating woman "urinating" blood. In tale 130 in which the girl is seized while kneading clay, we are presented with the inverse of this situation. There the girl retains waste fluids; she swells up and dies.

RML, tales   *71*   *130*

girl seized while throwing out *nixtamal*	=	girl seized while kneading clay
	(both softening functions)	

girl dies urinating lime water	or	girl swells up and dies
(evacuating waste)	≠	(retaining waste)

These women die from abnormal doses of sexuality: from *h?ik'al*'s six-foot penis, from multiple births, or from over-menstruating. In all these Zinacanteco tales about the Black-man, there is an equivalence between the crime that is committed and the punishment meted out. For example, Black-man cooks the blood of his victim (tales 67 and 71), whereupon he is caught and cooked; a man urinates on himself in fear of the Black-man, and *h?ik'al* is stabbed until his "filth ran out" (tale 123); a victim swells up and dies from being soaked in *h?ik'al*'s dark cave, and in this same tale *hʔikʾal* is kicked into the river (tale 130). In the tales of rape, the punishment usually has something to do with the offense, and the crime is one relating to sexuality.[10]As mentioned in section 1, female sexuality—especially when a woman is pregnant or menstruating (the manifest reverse of pregnancy)—is highly dangerous.[11] Unfortunately, no work has been done specifically on menstrual taboos and on what precautions are taken when a woman is menstruating. Nevertheless, there is data describing other instances where female pursuits embody danger to others and where women are called upon to exercise great precautions.

In both Zinacantan and San Pedro Chenalhó women are admonished to be careful while preparing corn. Zinacantecos believe that a woman who mishandles maize is subject to soul-loss (Vogt 1969). According to the Pedranos a famine known as *'ikʾal winal*[12] (*ʔikʾal viʔnal*) ("black hunger") is caused by women who are careless in grinding their corn and who allow pieces of meal to fall to the ground and be burned or stepped on (Guiteras-Holmes 1961:243). This attitude is reminiscent of the advice women receive at Christmastime from the *mamaletik*: "Wash the lime-soaked kernels well and take them to the mill!" (see chapter 2, part 2) The women are advised against going to the mill alone so that boys cannot accost them on the way. Another reason for a woman to not go out alone is that *hʔikʾal* will seize her. Again, women are called upon to safeguard their sexuality; rape or seduction would reflect on them as well as on their husbands and families. Female sexuality in general —especially when the women are in ambiguous conditions—and womanly tasks having to do with the preparation of corn are surrounded by dangers. The need for caution exists in both instances.

[10] This same correlation between sexual carelessness and punishment occurs in real life in Zinacantan; a girl who is overly flirtatious or careless with men is in danger of being gang-raped by a group of young men from the village.

[11] While I was writing this chapter, I received a letter from Victoria Bricker that describes the making of *chicha* at San Sebastian. The Alfereces make this ritual drink from large cylinders of *panela* (raw brown sugar). Before putting the cylinder in the pot it is important that it be bitten by pregnant women to keep it from spoiling.

[12] *ʔikʾal winal* derives from the same root *ʔikʾ* "blacks" as does *hʔikʾal* "Black-man" or *ʔikʾal* "the drops of blood from a baby's umbilical cord."

Women raped by *hʔikʼal* represent extremes in negligence. They are menstruating women who are preparing corn and who should thus be doubly cautious. Yet, when *hʔikʼal* arrives, they are sound asleep by the fire.

The most tantalizing ramifications of this hypothesis have to do with the ancient prototype of *hʔikʼal*, the Maya bat-demon who is associated with blood, sacrifice, and eroticism. As such, he would be an appropriate selection for the role Guiteras-Holmes designates as the "legendary chastiser of sexual sins." In addition, this bat-demon appears both to represent the extreme of the male ideal type —"hard"—and to be associated with female sexuality (or its exaggeration). This connection is best demonstrated by a passage from the *Chilam Balam* of Tizimín, Yucatán. "Sweet was the Ancient Fruit and succulent on the tongue; sweet to soften the hard heart; to mollify the angry passions, *Chac Vayab* the bat, he who sucks honey from the flowers." [Makemson 1951:42. See also chapter 3, part 2 for a discussion of bats and flowers].[13] In the myths, *hʔikʼal* is referred to as Strong-hand or Hairy-hand; otherwise, he asks his intended victims if *they* are strong or brave (RML, tale 124); the answer he gets to his challenge is, "Well, I'm brave. I'm man enough . . . ," which underscores the identification between strength, or hardness, and masculinity.[14] Though the Tzotzil word *ʦoʦ* "strong" sounds like the word *tsots* (or *soʦʼ*) "bat," there is no evidence (in the Laughlin Tzotzil dictionary) that the two are linguistically related (*ʦoʦ* also means "furry"; see p. 58).

The bat-demon has ancient connotations suggestive of hardness and super-masculinity that are apparently carried over into his contemporary manifestations as *hʔikʼal*. Although these connotations are somewhat extraneous to my argument, it is true for many parts of the world that the bat is associated with female sexuality and menstruation. For instance, in Europe it is believed that bats can recognize menstruating women. Among the Kogi of Colombia, a

[13] In the *Popol Vuh* the emblematic weapon of the bat-demon Camazotz is the staff "hardened by fire" (1950:149 n.3).

[14] One question that I have no answer for is whether the appellation Strong-hand, or Hairy-hand, has anything to do with an ancient epithet for the bat-demon, Grab-grab (Thompson 1966).

girl who has her first period is described as having been "bitten by the bat" (Reichel-Dolmatoff 1949–1950:270). Given the blood-sucking habits of the vampire, these beliefs are not surprising, but their prevalence does not mean that similar beliefs are held in Zinacantan. All that can be said with certainty concerning the ancient bat-demon and *hʔik'al* is that both are associated with blood and eroticism. The expression "ruined by the bat" is used by contemporary Zinacantecos to describe a deflowered virgin.

Because of the highly speculative nature of these last paragraphs I should perhaps summarize my arguments at this point, indicating where I shift to more tenuous ground.

1. The ancient bat-demon is associated with blood, death, sacrifice, and eroticism (see chapter 3).

2. Likewise, *hʔik'al* is connected with blood, death, punishment, and eroticism (see chapter 2).

3. It may be that *hʔik'al*, the "chastiser of sexual sin" (Guiteras-Holmes 1961), is a contemporary manifestation of the bat-demon.

4. In these tales about spooks from all over the Maya area, the spooks and their victims share an equivalent anomalous status (see chapter 5); furthermore, in the Black-man tales, the treatment dealt to a spook or to the spook's victims often reflects the offense committed.

5. More tentatively, the *nixtamal* in these myths is a euphemism for menstrual blood.

6. When *hʔik'al* seizes a woman at a task involved with cooking corn, and then kills her with an overdose of sexuality, I suggest that she is being punished for an underdose of care in her female responsibilities.

7. In order to depict a woman careless of her sexuality, Zinacantecos may choose the metaphor of a woman negligent during the times when she should be most careful—when she is cooking corn and when she is in an ambiguous condition, as during menstruation.

An anomaly is something unclassifiable in terms of usual categories. As suggested in the introduction, one way to deal with anomalies is to place them into their own category. In this way, the threat to culturally defined categories is eliminated. In addition, the categories of which the anomaly is not a member are clarified. There are several ways in which anomalies define norms; only one of these will be discussed here.

H?ik'al represents the ideal type of masculinity (hardness and potency) carried to a dangerous extreme, but at the same time he punishes those men in myths who are not hard enough and rewards those who live up to the ideal type (see part 1 of this chapter). In this instance, the ideal type (which I guess might be called "hardness in moderation") is bounded, and hence defined, by deviations from the norm.

punished by h?ik'al	*rewarded*	*h?ik'al is punished*
behavior that is too soft	correct behavior of a brave man	behavior that is too hard (exaggerated masculinity)
(man like a woman)		

At San Sebastian *h?ik'aletik* punish weak men and oversexed women and thereby define the ideal types for men and for women: men responsible in political office, women heedful of their sexuality. In the myths in which *h?ik'al* molests women, Black-man, who is himself super-sexed, punishes women who have failed to properly fulfill their sex-allocated role. By his own example and by the retributions he enacts, *h?ik'al* clarifies normative roles for men and women in Zinacantán.

> Rosemary ponders her baby:
> He *wasn't* a human being of course. He was some kind of half-breed . . . It would be so nice to look at him again if only he wouldn't open those animal yellow eyes . . . (Levin 1967)

3. Spooks and Babies

The most frequent dichotomies set up in the present analysis have been those between nature and culture, death and life; the spooks exist between the two poles, exhibiting attributes of both realms, belonging completely to neither. In order to disambiguate them, spooks are "cooked" or else treated with "civilizing" prescriptions like salt, lime, garlic, or tobacco. All these ingredients are used for "civilized" activities: lime is used in prepar-

ing corn (also, in mortar for houses); both liquor and salt are es-
sential components of ritual meals; garlic is used in curing; tobacco
is used in formal social relations. Cooking is a means of transforming nature into culture, or at least of clarifying the distinction. Likewise, ceremony would be a way of mediating between the living
and the dead. In the discussion that follows, the crucial point is that,
in the Tzotzil view, something can be transferred from one realm to
another by way of human processing.

Chapter 4, section 2, dealt with "Transforming Animals"—
the mouse that turns into a bat, the armadillo that becomes a turkey-
buzzard, the caterpillar that becomes a hummingbird. A fourth kind
of transformation that is perhaps less well known in Zinacantan is
that of the toad, ʔamuč, that becomes a dove, ṭuin (Acheson 1962:
46). These are all markedly terrestrial animals transforming themselves into creatures that fly, and it may be that some kind of mediation between earth and air is at work here. As was noted for San
Pedro Chenalhó (see fn. 5, this chapter), the foetus is also thought
to begin as a mouse. A month later it changes into a toad, and,
finally, during the third month, into a human infant. Does the
function of the transforming foetus also involve some kind of
mediation?

In Zinacantan, pregnancy and childbirth are classified as čamel
"body-sickness" (see fn. 4, this chapter). As with menstruating
women, women in this condition are both vulnerable and dangerous
to others. They have a grave responsibility to watch their behavior.
Insofar as pregnancy is the retention of blood, menstruation could
be said to be the opposite. Like nixtamal, menstrual blood may
be considered a form of waste—it is what has not been used to make
a baby. As waste, and as a manifestation of female sexuality, the
blood is ambiguous and potentially dangerous. In San Pedro Chenalhó, a menstruating woman may not come near where men are
burning lime because she would "blacken" the stones. If "blackening" is used here in the same sense as in the spook tales, it may have
to do with death, and also with rottenness. In other words, the
woman could cause the lime to putrefy before it can be burned.
Such an interpretation would be corroborated by Zinacanteco belief
that pregnant women cause fresh meat to putrefy. Special precau-

tions are necessary at the fiesta of *karnaval* in Chamula where women bite meat to forestall rotting and at San Sebastian in Zinacantan where they bite the cylinder of *panela* to save the *chicha* (see fn. 10, this chapter).

Significantly, the things that might be spoiled are all "raw" and about to be "cooked"—the meat, the *chicha*, and the lime that the men are burning. As was mentioned above, in connection with domesticating spooks, both cooking and ritual are modes of transforming nature into culture. The human foetus too may be "raw"; it is in the process of being "cooked" by its mother. At least, this is what is suggested by the analogy between the foetus and *atole*. A baby is not considered fully human until after baptism; in fact in Chamula the unbaptized baby is referred to as *maš*, or "little monkey" (personal communication from Gary Gossen). Its soul comes gradually and is not complete until fixed with salt at that ceremony.

Salt, of course, is part of the same treatment used to "civilize" a spook, and, like a spook, a foetus is between two poles. It is transitional between waste—an ambiguous non-living substance, on the outskirts of culture—and a live new human being. This opposition is most apparent in the differences between a menstruating woman and a pregnant woman. Both are dangerous to those around them, and both may cause fresh things to putrefy, but, while the waste that one exudes rots what it touches, the waste that the other retains is transformed into a baby. As something that is between two states, a foetus belongs to the set of anomalous substances ("set" as defined in the introduction). A foetus that does not complete the transformation—which is born dead—becomes a spook, the *špak'in te?*. It can hardly be a coincidence that *špak'in te?* is the spook whose sexual parts turn into excrement when exposed. The closest parallel to the Zinacanteco *špak'in te?* is the *xtabai* of Belize; she too is a demon with a hollow head or back who impersonates a sweetheart; she turns into rotten wood.

$$\text{person } (\textit{špak'in te?}) \longrightarrow \text{waste (excrement)}$$
$$\text{would be the inverse of}$$
$$\text{waste (menstrual blood)} \longrightarrow \text{person (baby)}$$

Provided that the postulates are correct, a set of categories reading waste → foetus → baby seems workable. An unborn baby would be somewhere between waste and human; an unbaptized baby would be transitional between something "rotten" and something "cooked." Like the transforming animals who mediate between earth and air, a foetus is non-living waste processed into a human being who mediates between nature and culture, death and life. It should be noted that diagrams, such as the one proposed here, are much less flexible than the symbols themselves whose multiple meanings play hopscotch with efforts to categorize them.

Dead	*In-between*	*Alive*
menstrual		fully formed
blood/waste	foetus	baby

Nature		*Culture*
"rotten"	unbaptized	"cooked"
non-person	person	person

vii. Apprehending Culprits

Even the analysis of synchronic structures requires constant recourse to history. By showing institutions in the process of transformation, history alone makes it possible to abstract the structure which underlies the many manifestations and remains permanent throughout a succession of events. (Lévi-Strauss 1963:21).

To the extent that *hʔikʼal* is feared as a bogie he is the enforcer of cultural norms, since myth and ritual affect real-life conduct. Tales about this axman on the look-out for deviant behavior also embody standards of correct behavior. In fact, nearly all the stories about *hʔikʼaletik* review characteristics implicit in "civilized" behavior.

Though the oppositions nature-culture, life-death, male-female may seem arbitrary or overencompassing, I think that a case has been made for their applicability in Zinacantan (see chapter 5). I use them here as armatures for some Zinacanteco categories that emerge from tales about anomalous categories and from the antics of *hʔikʼaletik* at San Sebastian and *karnaval*. In addition, in the Black-man tales and in the ritual activity involving *hʔikʼaletik*, certain ideal types for male and female behavior are depicted.

Table 18. Zinacanteco Categories Based on Opposition between Culture and Nature

	Culture	In-Between	Nature
Form and *attributes*	—human form	—human in animal form, with a tail, horns, shaggy hair, bad smell (like a buzzard), or with animal-like deformities	—animal form
Habitat	naetik (area under human control)	—paths, half-way up *cerro*, just outside village	—te?tik (wild area)
	—in the house	—doorways, eaves	—outside the house
Behavior	—"reasonable" (talking, arguing, knowing proper forms of speech and ceremonial etiquette, eating sociably; being monogamous, faithful, pious, industrious, etc.)	—ignoring norms (starving; being mute, promiscuous, lazy, blasphemous, adulterous, deceitful, incestuous, etc.)	—ignorant; incapable of "reasonable" behavior
Diet	—human food, e.g., tortillas	—waste material (corpses and excrement)	—animal food, e.g., flesh and excrement
		—burned food[1] (charcoal)	
	—food that is cooked or prepared	—half-baked food or food that is partially prepared (chicken with feathers on)	—raw food

[1] Robert Laughlin (personal communication) points out that burned food is a substance often placed in graves.

Table 19. Zinacanteco Categories Based on Opposition between Life and Death

	Life	In-Between	Death
Condition (applies to condition of the spooks' victims)	—body with flesh —warm body	—body without skin —body without flesh —putrefied body —cold limbs —shrivelled face —body that removes head —hollow back	—bare skeleton —dead cold
	—human baby —body with complete soul	—stillborn foetus (*špak'im teʔ*) —partial or temporary soul loss (*šiʔel*) as when drunk, asleep, sick, frightened, insane, etc.	—waste (menstrual blood) —complete soul-loss
Habitat	—in house	—cemeteries	—buried in grave

Table 20. Ideal Types Based on Opposition Male and Female

Male	Deviant	Female	Deviant
—a "hard" man who is brave and virile	—a woman who is "hard" or oversexed; a man who is "soft"	—a woman who is "soft" and submissive	
—a temperate man, strong enough to resist temptation, who fulfills cargo responsibilities	—a woman who is negligent in household responsibilities or who is careless with her sexuality; a man remiss in official duties or who is a drunkard	—a woman who is diligent in household tasks (e.g., cooking corn); heedful of her sexuality (who does not go out alone and who is careful not to endanger those around her)	

Long ago there were too many Black-
men. You couldn't go out alone.
(RML, tale 71)

1. An Unclosed Case

From the structural analysis of the tales, cer-
tain patterns emerge, which describe what sorts of people are anomalous and what becomes of them. As such, these patterns should
provide insight into Zinacanteco classification of behavior; the next
step must be to check these hypothetical categories. If the interpretations are valid, statements derived from them and retranslated
into Tzotzil parlance should be meaningful to Zinacantecos and
should provoke serious consideration and comment. One would
hope, for example, that a Zinacanteco would concur with the state-
ment that the woman who was asleep by the fire, who was murdered
by *hʔikʼal*, and whose blood boiled over has been careless in the performance of her duty. Eliciting a response, however, is a delicate
enterprise.

First, there is the problem of phraseology. The problem grows in
proportion to the degree of intellectual distance the interpreter has
indulged in. The closer the analysis has stayed to the Zinacanteco
idiom and cultural context, the easier the task of feedback will be;
still, it is optimistic to think that myths dissected in an academic
manner will retain their original fiber. The greatest problem in re-
couching the messages for feedback is that one misphrase may con-
taminate the meaning. In addition, there is the danger that the state-
ment will be a leading one, and that the germ of the response will
come from the retranslation.

In the case of *hʔikʼal*, the problem is even tougher. All myths
have multiple meanings, a fact that confounds interpretations; but
hʔikʼal is a symbolic figure (if he really is a bat-demon) whose distinguishing characteristics are euphemized beyond recognition. As
in the example I have cited before, Vogt's informant Domingo told
him: one must not say the name of the vampire bat or he will come.
Instead they call the bat ʔ*anhel*. In a generation, perhaps, people
will have forgotten that ʔ*anhel* meant "bat"; they will simply remember that these earth lords, or angels, or whatever the term will

designate, have sinister overtones. In the same way, the original identity of *hʔikʼal* may have been so camouflaged that it has been entirely forgotten. Only the euphemism and its connotations remain. The question arises: when euphemisms are so distant from their original referents, how valid is it to search for them? We must ask how the prototype tempers current meanings, or if it does so at all.

2. Missing Persons

The conclusion on feedback that I suggested in the preceding section must remain as a visionary chapter. Ideally such an ending would be written in Tzotzil and would include a series of statements that had been presented to Tzotzil informants along with their transcribed responses. Nevertheless, the reader has traveled far enough so that some itinerary is in order.

Nowhere in the myths or in other data collected from Tzotzil informants is it ever stated that *hʔikʼal* is related to a bat; as far as I know, no bat-demon exists for contemporary Zinacantan. Though he belongs to the set of anomalous creatures, *hʔikʼal* emerges as a non-transforming spook with animal characteristics, although he has no animal counterpart. Given the Tzotzil fascination for anomalous animals and the fact that they so often receive special attention in both myth and ritual, it is mysterious that the bat, with all the earmarks of an anomalous, transforming animal, is never mentioned in either context. At the other end of the argument, there is no evidence of Black-men as demons[1] in ancient Maya lore—though beliefs concerning the bat-demon were widespread.

The key to this mystery of the unmentioned demons is perhaps to be found in the euphemizing that is recorded for both Zinacantan and San Pedro Chenalhó. In order to keep fearful creatures at a distance, direct reference to them is traditionally avoided. Zinacantecos call the vampire *ʔanhel* (a name that probably designates "earth lord"). When speaking of the *ʼikʼal* (*hʔikʼal*), Pedranos substitute the expression "High Master." Could this intentional obfuscation

---

[1] There were, however, the soot-face Maya priests. Also, the murals at Bonampak depict somebody—both size and dress suggest a personage of distinction—whose whole body is (painted?) black.

be responsible for erasing references to the bat-demon in contemporary Zinacantan? Only the image—a winged super-sexed black bogie and its connotations—would remain. Not unreasonably, this demon might come to be called *hʔikʼal* "black man" (providing thus a convenient explanation for Black-man's color).

An alternative to this hypothesis is that the bat-demon has simply ceased to exist in Tzotzil imagining. Certainly much else has been lost (the loss of the ancient calendar system and the lost meaning of the glyphs are among the most famous examples). Still, a quick look shows that other animals like the jaguar, the hummingbird, and the vulture, which were likewise given primary attention by the ancient Maya, have maintained their status in contemporary myth and ritual. The turkey-buzzard, for example, behaves in myths today exactly like the ancient vulture, plucking out the eyes of human victims. Often these animals appear engaged in cosmic endeavors resembling the planetary struggles of ancient mythology; creatures are at war with, or defending, the Sun, Humanity, Evil.[2] In some of these instances *hʔikʼal* is a "new" insertion into otherwise much older contexts. For example, Pedranos describe how *tsʼunun* (*ṭʼunun*), the hummingbird, defends mankind against the jaguar and also against *ʼikʼal* (*hʔikʼal*). Similarly, in ritual, *hʔikʼaletik* appear in contexts reminiscent of much older ceremonies enacting themes of punishment and sacrifice; the props sported and the other characters involved also demonstrate relics from ancient times.

Two of the animals currently associated with the Tzotzil Black-man, the hummingbird (in San Pedro Chenalhó) and the buzzard, fall into a category of sky-diving creatures anciently associated with blood, sacrifice, and sexuality.[3] The ancient bat fits this description

[2] A discussion of the extent to which ancient symbols have retained their meanings through time would take us way beyond the evidence. As Early and others have pointed out, much has been lost. But how much? As was brought out in chapter 3, connotations marginal in one context can predominate in another, and small carry-overs can have a crucial influence. More importantly, we need to ask: when are similar meanings derived and when are they the result of parallel thinking? At best we can carry suggestions raised by the data to the guess stage.

[3] This connection between the ancient vulture and sexuality is a strained one, based only on a passing comment from J. E. Thompson 1932 (see page 66, this text). More definite evidence is available for Zinacantan today where he is associated with illicit sex and bad smell.

as well. In San Pedro the hummingbird, identified with the ancestor gods, is *hʔik'al*'s chief opponent. In Zinacantan two classes of hummingbirds are recognized, the daytime varieties and those which fly at night and carry messages from the ancestors and sickness from the witches. These invisible night-flying creatures may actually be confused with bats. Hummingbirds and bats sometimes compete for the same flower food source, which is possibly relevant to the association. According to one Zinacanteco informant, *hʔik'al* may himself be mistaken for a buzzard.

Curiously, all three of these volatile creatures—bat, hummingbird, and buzzard—are currently regarded by Zinacantecos as "transforming" animals involved in some earth-to-air transition. In addition, all three are somehow associated with eroticism or illicit sex—hummingbirds with male sexual prowess, buzzards with unwed mothers, the bat with deflowered virgins. Assuming that there is some carry-over between ancient and contemporary symbols, a filled-out model of missing persons reads as follows:

ancient (where all are sky-diving demons associated with blood, sacrifice, and eroticism)	*contemporary*
Vulture	Turkey-Buzzard* (punishment by gouging out eyes; illicit sex)
Hummingbird	Hummingbird* (eroticism)
Bat-Demon	Bat* (blood and eroticism) or *Hʔik'al* (blood, punishment, sexuality)

* Transforming animal

According to this model, there are no missing persons, only aliases; the *'ik'al* (*hʔik'al*) of San Pedro Chenalhó, who carries his victims off to Papasalenco and beheads them, and Camazotz of the *Popol Vuh*, who decapitates Hunahpu, would be one and the same culprit.

More modern candidates for Black-man than Camazotz exist, but it is unlikely that they provide the whole answer. The likeliest of these candidates include the "Moors" who battle "Christians" in a ceremony introduced into Middle America by the Spaniards, and Negro road-builders who worked in Chiapas some years ago. Laughlin provides linguistic evidence for the identification of *hʔik'al* with Moors: the Tzeltal word for sorghum, "moorish corn," is translated in Tzotzil as *tukum hʔik'al* "spook's corn." Similarly, *hʔik'al*'s kinky hair and the myth from Chamula that *hʔik'al* is a demon who feeds people to bulldozers supports an identification with the road-builders. It is important to note then that several sources may have contributed to Black-man's current identity, as congruous features were absorbed through time into the symbol for which the ancient bat-demon was probably the prototype.

Maya glyphs and codices depict a bat who is identified with death and sacrifice. If *hʔik'al* is indeed a contemporary manifestation of this demon, the emphasis has shifted from sacrifice to retribution. Whereas both creatures are associated with super-sexuality, the Black-man also deals out punishment for sexual sins. He is a deviant who punishes deviants, a "clarifying anomaly," working to define proper sex roles for men and women in Zinacantan.

At the Zinacanteco Christmas ceremony, characters known as *meʔ-čunetik* admonish women to behave well: to not go out alone and to perform household tasks diligently. "Wash the lime-soaked kernels well and take them to the mill. The girls must be accompanied by older women so that no boy will accost them." These *meʔ-čunetik* even dress up like women—though they continue to move and gesticulate like men—in order to show how ludicrous it is for someone in women's clothing to act like a man (Bricker 1968:206). In real-life Zinacantan, a girl who is particularly careless in such matters, who is too flirtatious, or who is independent to the point of masculinity, runs the risk of being gang-raped by a group of young men from the village.[4]

The preceding issues are focused upon in the Black-man myths.

---

[4] This practice—and also its reverse, where groups of women gang together and attack an offending male—is recorded in Zinacanteco myths collected by Bricker (1965–1966 Field Data).

Patterns that emerge from an analysis of the tales suggest that
hʔikʾal's victim who has fallen asleep while cooking corn is a negligent creature, comparable to the woman who goes out alone. The
woman who goes to "throw out the *nixtamal*" is a menstruating
woman not properly heedful of her own dangerous condition. Likewise, in ritual, *hʔikʾaletik* punish the wives of defaulting cargo
officials—women who supposedly are too strong or distractingly
oversexed. According to the jibes aimed at them, these women adopt
the male position in intercourse and like animals they copulate just
anywhere. These women have in common their failure to fill sex-
allocated roles; in each case their behavior has been inadequate or
else exaggerated. There is an analogy between these women and
the multi-potent boys who gang-rape an indiscreet girl. As seen
elsewhere in the spook tales, the punishment reflects the offense
committed. The right-hand column below, for creatures that are
"over-sexed," is for demons, but it could also include the people
punished by them: the wives of cargoholders or brazen women.

inadequate fulfillment of sex-role	"correct" behavior	exaggerated sexuality
careless or indiscreet females	diligent, modest, women careful of their sexuality	
		hʔikʾal
	virile but temperate males	men who commit rape

In general, *hʔikʾal* punishes women who are careless or who behave like men as well as men who behave like women. The distinction between humans and animals is crucial, since people who
ignore the criteria of "civilized" behavior are no less anomalous
than animals who seem to mimic humans or who are closely associated with them. This lumping of anomaly with anomaly is typical
of the logic underlying these tales and is the basis for talking about
a "set" of anomalous creatures. Included in the set are the spooks
themselves, their victims—who are humans in ambiguous conditions suffering from *šiʔel*, or partial soul-loss—their diet composed
of marginal substances like waste or corpses, the anomalous animals

like goats and dogs (at once domestic, scavenging, and free-ranging), and the marginal substances like excrement or rotten wood that they turn into.

Humans can be contaminated or endangered merely by exposure to this set, and special precautions are necessary. The man impersonating *h?ik'al* must stay awake; sleep would bring him too close to the spook's realm. People kidnapped by Black-man rarely return successfully to the human world: they die or turn into idiots. Civilizing ingredients (salt on food, tobacco at the doors) and procedures (like spoken prayers) delineate and reconfirm position within the category of human beings.

The existence of such a set of anomalies as well as the close fit between Black-man in myth, ritual, and real life supports the view that there is an underlying logic shaping events in all these contexts. This system may be ever-present, but it is also evasive and not always detectable through direct investigation. In myths it emerges only when the corpus is large enough so that patterns surface, or when comparative material, historical as well as contemporary, belonging to the same culture area (in this case the Maya region) illuminates them. When we do uncover this logic, we are in a position to make sense of seemingly senseless events. In the total framework of the culture, where myth, ritual, social norms, daily experience, and their interpretations all interact, these events bear meaning.

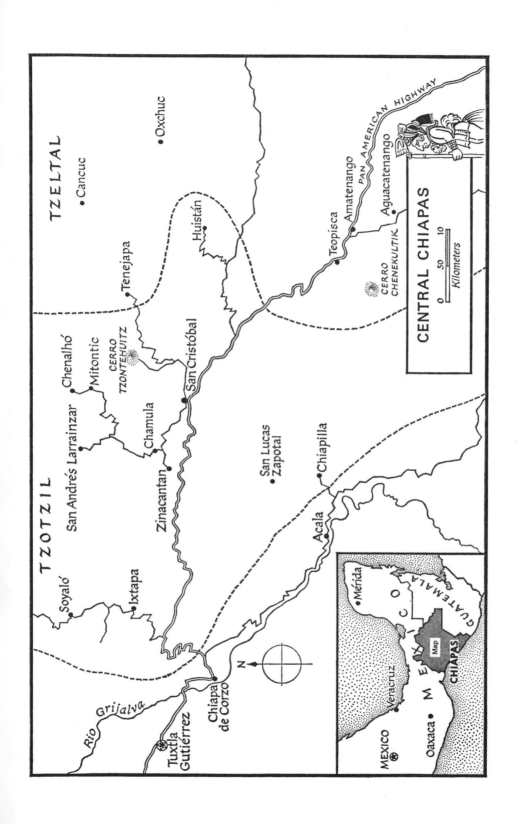

TZELTAL

• Cancuc
• Oxchuc

• Tenejapa
• Huistán

Chenalhó
Mitontic •
San Andrés Larrainzar
CERRO TZONTEHUITZ
• San Cristóbal
Chamula •

TZOTZIL

Soyaló •
• Ixtapa
Zinacantan

San Lucas
Zapotal •
• Chiapilla

• Acala

Rio Grijalva

Tuxtla Gutiérrez
Chiapa de Corzo

N

Teopisca
Amatenango

PAN AMERICAN HIGHWAY

Aguacatenango

CERRO CHENEKULTIK

CENTRAL CHIAPAS

Kilometers

0   50   10
Kilometers

Mérida •

G O L F O

MÉXICO
Veracruz •
Oaxaca •

M E X I C O

Map
CHIAPAS

GUATEMALA

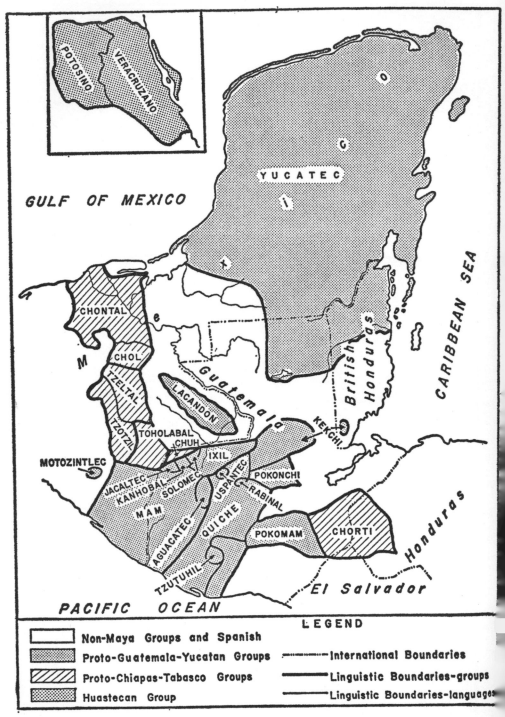

SCHEMATIC MAP OF DISTRIBUTION OF MAYA-SPEAKING INDIANS.

CHAMA'

SANTIAGO CHIMALTENANGO

STO. TOMAS
CHICHICASTENANGO

STA. CATARINA
IXTAHUACAN

NAHUALA'

STA. LUCIA UTATLÁN

PANAJACHEL

S. ANTONIO PALOPO'

LAKE ATITLÁN

S. PEDRO LA LAGUNA

SANTIAGO ATITLÁN

SAMAYAC

CHINAUTLA

GUATEMALA

LAKE AMATITLÁN

GUATEMALA AND
THE TOWNS AROUND
LAKE ATITLÁN

Scale:

0   5   10   20   30

LAKE ATITLÁN

GUATEMALA

The dwarf *Huasanga*, riding *Cadejo*, the *Sigua-monta*, *Siguanaba*, *Siguapate*, the *Weepweep-weeping woman* . . . such different demons! . . . legions of shadow-makers, endemonized people, necromancers, astrologers . . . sorcerers.

(Asturias 1967)

APPENDICES: Legions of Shadow-Makers

APPENDIX I: Index of Spooks and Sources[1]

Black-Man (*Hʔikʼal*)
  Zinacantan (Tzotzil)
          —RML, tale 23
          —RML, tale 25
          —RML, tale 67
          —RML, tale 71
          —RML, tale 122
          —RML, tale 123
          —RML, tale 126
          —RML, tale 130
          —VRB 106 x072
          —EZV F-I 8
  San Pedro Chenalhó (Tzotzil)
          —Guiteras-Holmes
              1961:248, 299–300
  Chamula (Tzotzil)
          —Arciniega 1947:473–474
  Oxchuc (Tzeltal)
          —Villa Rojas 1946:309–310

Brujos
  Zinacantan (Tzotzil)
          —RML, tale 4
          —RML, tale 62
          —RML, tale 32
          Bricker 1968:179–180

[1] I visited Yucatán the spring of 1967; I spent the summers of 1966 and 1967 working on medical projects in Guatemala and Honduras. References to Blaffer are to talks I had during these travels. Kay Kreiss was a co-worker.

San Antonio, Belize (Kekchi)
    —Thompson 1930:158
Santa Lucia Uxtatlan (Quiché)
    —Blaffer 1967
Yucatán (Yucatec)
    —Castillo 1965

Buzzard-Man (Šulem Vinik)
  Zinacantan (Tzotzil)
    —RML, tale 42
    —RML, tale 48
    —RML, tale 62
  San Pedro La Laguna (Tzutujil)
    —Paul 1962:91
    —Rosales 1949:621
    —Tax 1950:2543
  San Pedro Chenalhó (Tzotzil)
    —Guiteras-Holmes 1961:204

Cadejo
  Agua Escondida (Tzutujil?)
    —Redfield 1945:35, 195–196
  Santa Lucia Uxtatlán (Quiché)
    —Blaffer 1967
  Santo Tomás Chichicastenango
    (Quiché)
    —Tax 1947:469
    (Chorti)
    —Wisdom 1940
  Samayac (Quiché)
    —Blaffer 1967

Characotel
  San Pedro La Laguna (Tzutujil)
    —Paul 1947:297, 3859–3860
                3863–3865
                3877–3884
                3937–3953
  Agua Escondida (Tzutujil)
    —Redfield 1945:35, 49, 195–197
  Panajachel (Cakchiquel)
    —Tax 1950:2560, 2561

Santa Lucia Uxtatlán (Quiché)
    —Blaffer 1967
Samayac (Quiché)
    —Blaffer 1967

Charcoal-Cruncher
Zinacantan (Tzotzil)
      —RML, tale 12
      —RML, tale 47
      —RML, tale 60
      —RML, tale 81
      —VRB 1965–1966 x075

Corpse-Eater
Zinacantan (Tzotzil)
      —RML, tale 73
      —RML, tale 4

El Güin or *Win*
Santa Lucia Uxtatlán (Quiché)
    —Blaffer 1967
Samayac (Quiché)
    —Blaffer 1967
Santiago el Palmar (Quiché)
    —Saler 1967:79–83
Finca Ascensión (Quiché)
    —Told to Blaffer by Kay Kreiss 1967

Lab
Cancuc (Tzeltzal)
    —Guiteras-Holmes 1946:141, 150, 268

Lechura or *Lechuza*
San Andrés Tuxtla
    —Starr 1950:iii
Finca Ascensión (Quiché)
    —Told to Blaffer by Kay Kreiss 1967

Nagual
Nebaj (Ixil)
    —Lincoln 1945:38

Siguanaba
Santa Lucia Uxtatlán (Quiché)

—Blaffer 1967
—Wisdom 1940:407
—Asturias 1967:110

Sirena
  Agua Escondida (Tzutujil?)
            —Redfield 1945:35, 49

Split-Faced Man
  Zinacantan (Tzotzil)
            —VRB

White Bundle
  Zinacantan (Tzotzil)
            —Zabala Field Data 1957–1959:10

Xpakinte, or *Špak'in te*?
  Zinacantan (Tzotzil)
            —EZV Interview 1960–1962:71–78
            —Laughlin 1963–1969
  Chamula (Tzotzil)
            —Arciniega 1947:473–474
  Cancuc (Tzeltzal)
            —Guiteras-Holmes 1946:39

Xtabai
  San Antonio, Belize (Kekchi)
            —Thompson 1930:157
  Yucatán
            —Blaffer 1967

APPENDIX II: Catalogue of Spooks from the Maya Area

A. Humans who turn into animals

B. Humans who shed their skin, or flesh, or take off their heads, spirits in human form and Black-men

> The question posed is if a man can defeat the Flesh-eating Mule since a man too is a flesh-eating beast, except on days of abstinence—'very rational, but very meat-eating.' (Asturias 1967)

A. Humans Who Turn into Animals

The spook-tale pattern most prevalent in the Maya area is one in which human beings transform themselves into animals, especially domestic animals, like dogs, goats, mules, and pigs, although they may also become wild animals, such as tigers, tapirs, and coyotes. When a bird is involved, it is often an owl, or else a large scavenger or carrion-eater, like a buzzard. The spooks that follow this pattern are the *güin*, the *characotel*, the *cadejo*, and the *lechuza* of Guatemala, as well as some of the witches reported from British Honduras, Chiapas, and Yucatán. Though he is not a spook (an *espanto* that frightens people) I include here Buzzard-man, a character well known throughout Mexico and Central America.

These spooks turn into animals, and are characterized by animal behavior and attributes. They steal chickens, eat carrion, and whisk people away. Often they behave promiscuously. These spectres carry illness and death. Hooves, horns, tails, or shaggy hair are among their spook accoutrements. Like domestic animals, *characoteles* may wear a chain, a rope, or a bell around their necks. *Characoteles*, especially buzzard-men, are notorious for their bad smell. Usually these spooks are black, but they may also be white or red, and they may have frightening red or yellow eyes that glisten in the night. These spooks are special from birth, though people around them may not recognize at once their peculiar powers. Sometimes, a spook will be born with a veil, and then "people will know" that it is a spook. In San Pedro la Laguna it is reported that a husband once found out that his wife was a *characotel* and that her parents agreed to take her back.

Usually there is some ritual necessary in order for the spooks to change their forms—rolling on the ground, turning around (*dando vueltas*), removing the head or flesh or clothes, then rolling or turning, and so on. They change shapes in forest clearings, behind doors, and beneath crosses. Before going off into the night, the spook may make tests to be certain that the family is asleep. For example, a *characotel* wife pinches the nose of her husband and children, or else steps over them several times; she may also stick her rump in her sleeping husband's face.

To punish a spook, to destroy it, or else to permanently seal it into its animal form, the husband or wife throws a special concoction on it, such as salt, or else steals its clothes. There are special sticks of *chichicaste* for beating *characoteles*, as well as certain humans who possess magic properties for domesticating them.

The name *characotel* is found only in Guatamala; most of my information comes from the state of Sololá. Though people in the coastal state of Suchitepequez seem to know what the *characotel* is, they will add, "but it isn't here." The *characotel*, however, resembles some of the Suchitepequez examples of man-to-animal transformations, and its attributes are probably confused at times with those of the *cadejo* and the *güin*, spooks that are considered more local.

The distinguishing feature of a *characotel* is the chain or rope that hangs around its neck. In San Pedro la Laguna, a *characotel* may wear a corncob that is really a bell, or the leader of a band of *characoteles* will wear a bell. The *characotel* is always a domestic animal, especially a dog or a goat, and the chain around the neck appears to emphasize its connection with men. This closeness to men is emphasized by exaggeratedly polite behavior. In San Pedro la Pedro, the *characotel* takes its hat off to a person. Generally, the behavior of a *characotel* is anti-social. It robs, carries illness, or impersonates a relation. In San Pedro la Laguna, *characoteles* are said to smell like buzzards.

Closely related to the *characotel* is the *cadejo*. In Samayac and Aqua Escondida, the two are considered to be the same spook. Nevertheless, there do seem to be differences. For instance, I have never heard of a *cadejo* who becomes a goat. Although he is normally a domestic animal, both Asturias and Wisdom mention a *cadejo* who is associated with a jaguar. Usually *cadejo* is a dog, especially a shaggy dog, and, of course, the word *cadejo* means "entangled hair." Among the Chorti, *cadejo* has long plaited hair; Asturias says he has a mane and calls him the "animal with the skin of a hairy river."

In Agua Escondida, *cadejo*, like *characotel*, may wear a chain around his neck, which may be due to a blending of traits between two similar spooks; elsewhere, there is no mention of anything worn around *cadejo*'s neck.

In Samayac, and in Santa Lucia Uxtatlán, *cadejo* is known for taking care of drunks. *Cadejo* also seems to have a connection with crosses; it may wear one on its forehead, and if a person passes *cadejo*, he should quickly make the sign of the cross with the left hand. The *güin*, according to people of the inland state of Sololá, is a spook of the coast; it is a man who turns into an animal, especially a dog, in order to steal chickens. To transform itself, the *güin* makes a trip to the cemetery, where it leaves its clothes at the foot of a cross, and rolls over three times.

Information about the *lechuza*, or *lechura*, is scarce. It is a witch that changes itself into some kind of animal, or, especially, into a bird. In Chinautla, Guatemala, a *lechuza* is a charmed person and an invisible thief who turns into an owl. It can be heard whistling as it flies about at night.

Stories about the *lab* are reported only from Cancuc. It may be the "size of a horse," have horns, or otherwise be a rat. It is a type of *nagual* that may become a billy-goat, a squirrel, a rat, a buzzard, or a cat. It lives in the Laguna of the Cerro Grande, appearing only when there is a strong current, or else it lives in a cave. It comes around whenever anyone is sick.

The spooks that I classify here as *brujos* are simply those which fit the man-to-animal description without having any special name. These witches may transform either themselves or their victims into domestic animals, like dogs, cats, cows, goats, pigs, or horses; into wild animals; or into birds, either owls or buzzards. These witches bring illness and death. Whether they eat excrement or carrion or, in one case, bats, or whether they eat nothing and starve, there is apt to be something strange about their diet. They take part in the rituals typical of transform-spooks: they remove their heads or skin or flesh, roll on the ground, move in circles, and so forth.

The *naguales*, like the Nabaj men who change themselves into animals in order to kill chickens and turkeys, seem to be a generalized version of the same kind of spook. Though the use of the term *nagual* is widespread in Middle America, the concepts it refers to are so complex that I have not included it with spooks in my survey. It should be pointed out, however, that the belief in *naguales* and in the ability of some men to turn themselves into animals goes deep in the Maya past. *Tecum Uman*, an ancient king of the Quiché Maya, was supposed to have been a great sorcerer who flew over his armies in the form of a Quetzal bird. Núñez de la Vega, bishop of Chiapas in the late seventeenth century, records the power of certain individuals to change into jaguars or balls of fire.

The final character in this group of men who become animals is Buzzard-man. Although he does not fit into the patterns of spook behavior, he does turn into a bird, and he does eat carrion. Like the *bruja* stories, the tale of Buzzard-man has a wide distribution in the Maya area, and versions of it are told in northern Mexico as well. Buzzard-man is a lazy farmer who yearns for an easier life, like that of a buzzard. He would like to have nothing to do except fly about looking for carrion, and finally he switches identities with the bird.

As widespread as the tale is the folklore that buzzards stink "like a man who has been working." It is this bad odor that gives the Buzzard-turned-man away. Another frequent theme is the man-turned-buzzard who burns himself up while searching for food, because, as the Buzzard advises his counterpart, "where you see smoke, there is a meal." Another man-to-bird transformation that is spoken of in Zinacantan is the unfaithful, lazy husband who becomes a bird called the *k'us ṭukutin*: "When they [his relatives] saw that he was doing something bad," the man became a bird.

> But the shape is not important,
> it's the stink—right, Mr. Cadejo?
> (Asturias 1967)

B. Humans Who Shed Their Skin or Flesh or Take Off Their Heads; Spirits in Human Form and Black-men

Even spooks who do not actually change into animals often possess animal attributes or attributes that are considered animallike. They smell "like a buzzard," they are promiscuous "like a dog," or they eat corpses like some scavenger animal. These spooks are closely associated with animals by their habitats, behavior, and diets. They ride through the night clinging to animals, or else parts of their bodies may attach to animals. In some cases, they may be protectors of a class of animals.

They are dehumanized beings who discard skin or flesh and leave their homes in order to attend private ceremonies or dig up carrion. They are the disembodied heads that go off into the night to crunch charcoal, to carry illness, and to frighten people. They may be humans who turn into demons, or demons who take on human form, like the female impersonators who haunt the evening roads hoping to lure men into the forest.

Among these tales of dehumanized beings, stories of devils and Black-men seem out of place simply because they are spooks who never pretend to be human and who do not change shape. Nevertheless, they inhabit the same ambiguous world, part way between the animal and the human, which seems to qualify them as dehumanized.

The Charcoal-cruncher as a "personality" is apparently unique to Zinacantan. There are no tales recorded elsewhere about wives (and sometimes husbands) whose disembodied heads take off at night to go chew carbon. Nevertheless, the Charcoal-cruncher frequents spook habitats and indulges in common spook behavior with

all the excuses spooks commonly make to explain strange absences
and cold faces ("I have been out to urinate," etc.). Like his carrion-
eating counterparts, he partakes of strange fare. As with some
transform-witches, Charcoal-cruncher's head may become attached
either to the spouse (making him two-headed) or to an animal. Like
other spooks, he is susceptible to salt, which seals him out of his
human form. In one case, hot water is thrown on the Charcoal-
cruncher—a punishment often dealt to Black-men.

Zinacantan hosts another uncommon spook, who is recorded in
Bricker's field notes as Split-faced man. He is a devil and a murderer whose face is split—half-white, half-black. Like other spooks,
he is hard to kill; he finally succumbs to a concoction of garlic, salt,
and tobacco.

Unlike Charcoal-cruncher, *h'ik'al* is widely known and feared
throughout Chiapas. Although Negro road-builders working in
Chiapas may have had some bearing on his black skin and curly
hair, his roots probably go much deeper in time. In Chamula,
Black-man has two aspects. He is a *pukuh*-type demon who carries
people off in order to feed them to road-building machines. He is
also the cosmic opponent of Sun and Moon who is out to destroy
humanity. Similarly, in San Pedro Chenalhó, *h'ik'al* struggles
against the hummingbird, 'Ts'unun (*t'unun*), who is mankind's
preserver; again, the fight has cosmic overtones.

Further complicating the role of *h'ik'al* is the part he plays in
fiestas in many parts of the Maya area. Whether his role is a per-
version of the Spanish mock-battle between Christians and Moors
or of ancient Maya connotations attached to the winged black
demon, or whether he is just a composite of symbols that suit men's
sense of demon construction, he is a yearly protagonist in Maya-
Christian ceremonies in the fiestas of San Andrés in Oxchuc, *karnaval* in San Pedro Chenalhó, and San Sebastian and *karnaval* in Zinacantan. (Characters labelled "negritos" also appear in ceremonies in
the towns around Lake Atitlán in Guatemala.) Usually, Black-
man's role in these ceremonies is to chastise sexual excesses.

The most detailed accounts of *h'ik'al* appear in Laughlin's
corpus of myths from Zinacantan. In these myths, he is a small,
black-skinned, curly haired demon with wings on his feet (or on his

knees) and a six-foot-long penis. Incredibly potent, his offspring begin to appear three days after conception and appear continually thereafter. He steals chicken eggs, fowl, and bread, but never tortillas. His prowling time is at dusk, and he often makes his home in caves.

Stories about the *h²ik'al* in Zinacantan follow several outlines. Among the most common is the one that begins with some form of "long ago there were too many Black-men." A woman will be cooking corn by the fire and fall asleep. Before drifting off, however, she will call to a comadre to wake her when her corn is boiling. While she sleeps, the *h²ik'al* arrives and murders her. When the neighbor calls, "Your corn is boiling over," it is actually the dead woman's blood hissing on the fire. When the comadres discover her death, they band together to punish Black-man. They offer him coffee or chicken broth and then proceed to scald him with it. They cook him "like a chicken." Afterwards, they may even skewer and roast him and chop his carcass to bits. So common is this tale that a sputtering on the fire has become a household synonym for Black-man's presence.

The remaining spooks, corpse-eaters, and impersonators are familiar ones. The Skeleton-woman (in a tale recorded by Laughlin) resembles the transform-witches of the first group. Instead of turning into an animal, however, she leaves her flesh behind the door in order to go to the cemetery and eat corpses. When her husband puts salt on the discarded flesh, she must remain as a skeleton, and, finally, with "no words, she died . . ." This Skeleton-woman does not argue like a normal wife; she does not eat human food in the company of her husband and family, but eats corpses while alone in the cemetery. She grows thin and her face gets ugly and shrunken. In behavior and aspect, she becomes progressively dehumanized until, finally, she dies.

As spook tales go, the witch account recorded by Moises Castillo is a classic. The sorceress leaves her skin and clothes behind to go off to a clearing in the woods, where she indulges in a private ritual. One evening her husband follows and overhears the strange cries muttered at midnight beneath the ceiba tree. He puts salt on her skin and she is unable to return to her human identity.

Siguanaba is either half-snake, half-woman, or a demon who impersonates lovers. She has long hair and wears white clothes. Though she may be described as either pretty or very ugly, it is always agreed that her face is hidden. She is associated with water and streams, and she deposits her victims in the barranca. According to the Chorti version, she will drive the man she seduces mad; she carries children off only to return them insane. Like *hʔik'al*, she especially chooses drunks for victims. According to Asturias' account of her, *siguanaba* recognizes what her prospective victims have been drinking by the wind they break.

In Agua Escondida, *sirena* is the same as *siguanaba*. Like *siguanaba*, *špak'in teʔ* takes on the guise of a woman in order to lure men, especially travelers, into the middle of the forest. The *xtabai* also impersonates sweethearts. In Yucatán, she is called *xcit cheel* and is associated with the ceiba tree. She wears a white huipil and may be seen combing her long hair. In a tale from British Honduras, *xtabai* walks backwards to conceal her rough hollow back. If her victim discovers that she is an impersonator and begins to pray, the *xtabai* will turn into a heap of rotten wood.

All over Mexico and Guatemala there are tales about the wailing woman called *la llorona*. She can be anything from the ghost of Cortes' mistress to a mother lamenting her lost child. The finca Ascensión version of this spook is not typical. There, *la llorona* turns into a monster two-tailed serpent. If a man encounters her at midnight at rivers, or at crossroads, she sticks her tails into his nostrils and squeezes.

APPENDIX III: Tales of *h²ik'al* from Zinacantan[1]

A. Tales of *h²ik'al* molesting women:
  1. RML, tale 71 (Chapter 2)
  2. RMR, tale 122 (rubic to Chapter 2)
  3. RML, tale 23– The Spook (*h²ik'al*)
  4. RML, tale 67–The Spook (*h²ik'al*)
B. Tales of *h²ik'al* accosting travelers:
  1. EZV Field Interview-8
  2. RML, tale 123– The Black-man and the Girl from Magdalenas (Chapter 2)
  3. RML, tale 124– The Chamula and the Spook (*h²ik'al*)
  4. RML, tale 126– The Spook (*h²ik'al*) and the Girl from San Andrés
  5. RML, tale 127–The Spook (*h²ik'al*) and the Brothers-in-law
  6. RML, tale 125– The Man Who Took the Spook's Wings.
C. Tales of *h²ik'al* asking for children:
  1. RML, tale 68– The Spook (*h²ik'al*) and the Saints
  2. RML, tale 130– Black-man Asks for Children (Chapter 2)
D. Miscellaneous:
  RML, Dream 190– I Dream of the Spook

THE SPOOK (*h²ik'al*)

The people went into caves. There were many spooks long ago. They say that there was [a woman] who had a comadre. They called back and forth. "Your corn has boiled over," she told her comadre.

She didn't answer. The spook spoke, the spook answered, "The corn is hissing, comadre." It was human blood. The comadre of the one who had been speaking died when she was grabbed inside her house. [The other woman] heard the spook answer. That person in her house was scared.

Quickly they went into their caves, they hid inside caves. That's how the people stayed alive in the olden days. Long ago there were

---

[1] Tales cited here appear in this appendix unless they appear in the text.

many spooks. [The people] knew how to save up their farts. That was what they gave the spooks. That was how they defended themselves from the spooks. They stayed there until dawn. There were many spooks long ago. Many died long ago because of the people-eaters.   (RML, tale 23)

THE SPOOK (*h^ʔik'al*)

Once there were many spooks, long ago. Many too many spooks long ago. There weren't many people at all. There were few people—just women.

It was night time when the spooks arrived. There were many of them. They came to eat. That's what they did. The spooks came to eat.

One came, one arrived. There was a neighboring house nearby, [near] where the spook killed someone, killed that woman. It seems she was asleep next to the fireside. The fire was already hissing with her blood.

Now the other house was nearby. She lived nearby, like in a room next door. "Comadre, your corn boiled over," she said, for she thought that [her comadre] was making corn gruel, that she had boiled the corn. But no, it was her friend's blood. "Your corn boiled over," she said. Because [her comadre] had boiled corn, boiled it. That's what the other [woman] thought. Since she lived nearby, that's what she thought, that the corn pot had turned over and spilled. But no, it was her friend's blood.

The spook answered. "The corn is ready, comadre," said the spook.

"It has spilled over, it has spilled over, comadre, your corn has spilled over," said her friend.

The spook answered. "The corn is ready, comadre," said that spook, you see.

He went away. She died. That woman died. That was the end of her.

He went, he went another night. All the women gathered together. They moved into one house. Now they weren't apart. Each house had been separate. There weren't many people at all. Just spooks were abroad then. They gathered together one night. "But the devil will come tonight," they said. For the women were strong-hearted. They cooked a meal for him. They cooked a chicken. The broth was good.

The spook arrived. "Will you eat? Eat!" they told him.

"Well, I could eat," said the spook.

"Well, drink lots of broth, please drink the broth! There is broth," said the women. When they saw that he was drinking the broth, when his face was hidden a bit, then they threw the broth on him. It was very hot. They killed the spook. They killed him. The spook died. He died. He died from the boiling water, but it was broth. They spilt broth, sprinkled it, spilt it. The women gathered together. They used boiling water on the others. They boiled it another time. They threw lots on them. They died from the boiling water. That was the end of the spooks.   (RML, tale 67)

EZV Interview with Domingo de la Torre Perez
March 5, 1960, p.2

One time in Tierra Caliente—one or two men slept on the Cerro de San Lucas and put their cargo down off their horses. Then the man had an escopeta. He woke up and saw an *hʔikʼal* eating his beans by the fire, so took his escopeta and shot the *hʔikʼal* through the chest. He didn't fall right there, but started to fly through the air so he shot him again. When dawn came the man went to see where the *hʔikʼal* was sitting down, the place where he had been shot. They talked and the *hʔikʼal* said he had not been killed, the man said he was going to shoot him again unless he gave him all the money that he had. So *hʔikʼal* gave the man several thousand pesos, and then the man shot and killed him! He proceeded to examine the body to see how he could fly. Couldn't find any wings, but finally found something behind his feet which permitted him to fly. He took them off the *hʔikʼal*, put them on his own feet, and went off flying a great distance because the little wings, or whatever they were, wanted to take the man off to the pueblo of the *hʔikʼal*. When he wanted to rest, he took off these things and threw them

away. And the man came home on foot, and picked up his load and
came on home.   (FI-8)

THE CHAMULA AND THE SPOOK (*hʔik'al*)

There was a Chamula who met a spook on the trail. "Well, friend,
where are you going?" asked [the spook].

"Sir, I'm going home," he replied. The sun was about to set.

"Aha! [And] where is your home?" he asked.

"Here," said [the Chamula].

"Forget your home, bastard, let's fight," said [the spook].

"Well, the filth of your mother's cock! If you are a spook, hell,
we'll see how it turns out," the Chamula said.

"Well, fine, if you're brave," the spook said.

"Well, I'm brave. I'm man enough if you're man enough," said
[the Chamula]. The fight began. Hell, he didn't delay. Right away
the spook was slugged. [The spook] didn't last a half hour. The
Chamula prayed the vespers, but the whorish spook probably never
prayed the vespers.

Well, it didn't take even a half hour for the Chamula to give
him a good stab. He finished pulling off his wings, the spook's
wings that were [attached to] his knees.

You see, the fucking Chamula said, "What would happen if I
stuck them on my legs?" He finished sticking them on his knees,
one after another. He stood up. He tried to fly. He tried to fly. The
second time he didn't rise up. The third time he went on and on.
The wings carried him. He went as far as the land of the spooks.

"Well what are you looking for?" he was asked by the lady
spooks, by [the spook's] brothers, fathers, and mothers. "But is it
because you killed my son?" they asked.

"No, not at all, I gave him eggs to eat, because I'm feeding him.
He is waiting for me to return again," he said.

"Are you telling the truth?" they said.

"Yes," he replied.

He went very far, for the wings carried him. He stuck them on
his knees here, one after another. The wings were of yellow metal,
this long. I have seen them. I have seen them. I saw one there to the

east, there probably where the red door is [in a store in the main square of San Cristóbal]. Mark [?] brought it.

That Chamula stuck them on, stuck them on here. He tried to fly. At first he just crashed. The second time [he went] this far. The third time he flew. Before he realized it, he had landed in the spooks' country. He arrived exactly at the spook's house. You see the wings carried him along.

"What are you looking for?" they said. "Where is my child? Have you killed him?" they asked.

"I never killed him, for I am feeding him. He is waiting for me at home too," he said.

"Well, we'll go leave you," they said. I don't know what country it was where they went to leave him. He was given this much jerked meat. "Go, eat it on the way. When you arrive give it to my son. Take care of him. We want him to come [home]. I don't want you to kill him."

"No, he has always been my friend because we travel together," said the Chamula, so that he could be freed. God, don't believe it, the [spook's] flesh had already dried up.

Well, but the fucking Chamula . . . "His money?" they asked.

"Oh but you can't think I'm looking for his money for him since he really has taken it with him," said the Chamula. In the place where they had fought, there in his tracks, he quickly buried it in the ground. He didn't take it, lest it be stolen. It would grow dark on the way. If you come to change it here [in San Cristóbal] right away, [they would say] "Where did you find it, where is your invoice?" If you come to change it they don't want you to deposit it. Hold it in your tunic, look at it every few minutes. Come change it that way. But if you lose it from sight, it will just [turn into] black potsherds.

You see there where the fucking spook had left his several thousand [pesos] buried, they were left buried.

When he looked, the Chamula arrived [in the land of the spooks]. Who knows where the spook's land is. "But what are you doing?" Their child was already bones. Nothing happened to [the Chamula]. He won.

"Well, I'll keep my child's wings here," they said.

"What filth of your mother's cock! How come you are going to keep your child's wings? How is your son to come [back] again? I'm taking them back to him," he said. He was allowed to come [home]. Now [the wings] didn't stick on. He just carried them. Who knows how many days it took him to arrive in Chamula country. He went to look at the money. The money was just the same, since it was buried. Some Chamulas are right smart. The spook was well screwed.   (RML, tale 124)

THE SPOOK (*hʔikʼal*) AND THE GIRL FROM SAN ANDRÉS

Once there were two men who went to the lowlands. The sun set [before] the men [reached their destination]. They slept by the path at ʔAnob.

Night fell and they slept on the side of the trail. Well, when night fell one of them had chills. He just had chills. He was shivering and quaking from the cold. "Oh, hell, I don't know why I'm shivering so from the cold. I don't know if something is going to happen to us tonight," he told his friend.

"Hell, what are you doing? Hell, aren't you a man? Haven't you any balls?" [the other one] said to his friend. One of them was brave, one was. "What are we scared of? Hell, do you think something is going to come?" that one said. [The other] didn't answer.

When night fell, the moon was bright. A terrific wind came. It was very strong. Now they saw him. It was quite late at night. Gliding along he arrived, carried by the wind he arrived. He landed at the foot of a big tree. Now as for our friends [our fellow Zinacantecs], they were sleeping happily.

After he arrived he was squatting at their fireside. "In the name of God what can I do about it now?" one of them said. [The spook] came [closer]. Both of them had certainly seen him. The other one [who had spoken bravely] just slept. He was helpless. Now when [the spook] arrived, the one [who had been scared] quickly shot at him.

[The spook] left. He flew off. He landed in a gully. Now [the man] said to his friend, "Hurry up, bastard! What are you doing? Whoever heard of such a thing? So it's just your mouth talking to yourself. You didn't tell the truth—that you are brave," he told that friend of his. The fellow was told, the one who had said back in Zinacantan center, "Are you brave?"

Well, then, that's the way it was. He just killed [the spook]. He just shook [his friend], but his friend was helpless. So he killed [the spook] by himself in the gully.

Now when he returned he had already killed the spook. He came to the fireside. He came to shake his friend. They went. His friend woke up. They went to look at what had landed at the foot of the tree. They went to look. There was a straw mat. Something was rolled up inside the straw mat. "Hell, what could it be? Come on, let's untie the straw mat," the two men said to each other.

They untied it. You know what? They found a San Andrés girl there. They took the San Andrés girl with them. They went and lit their fire for her. They let her warm up. They gave her tortillas. They fed her. They slept with her.

Now they came. They came up [to Zinacantan]. "God, where are you from?" they asked the girl.

"Ah, I'm from San Andrés. I was caught by a spook, because I went out to pour out my *nixtamal* water," she said "When I went outside the spook caught me. It was he who carried me here. So won't you please take me back," said the girl

"OK, why not?" those men told her.

They went, went to leave her in San Andrés. Then they arrived and met her father. "God, thank you friends. Thank you. May God repay you for bringing my daughter back to me. She was taken off by a spook," said the gentleman.

Our friends [our fellow Zinacantecs] delivered the girl. "Well, thank you, friends. Thank you. Here is your payment. Here is your meal. Drink a little!" they were told. The men were given drinks in thanks for having returned the girl it seems. So that's how the girl returned. She got home. That's how it ended.   (RML, tale 126)

The Spook (*hʔikʼal*) and the Brothers-in-Law

Once there was a man who went to Chamula. On the way back he met his brother-in-law on the trail. "Let's drink, brother-in-law," he said. He and his brother-in-law got drunk. They came along drunk.

They passed by Søeleh Minaš, they went on, because the man's house was in Na Čih.

They went beyond Na Čih. A comadre of his brother-in-law had a house there. "Comadre, won't you sell me a fourth or a half [bottle of cane liquor] or so?" he said, because she was a shaman [and would have left-over cane liquor].

His comadre [answered], "Take it, compadre, take it. Do you just want a half."

"Just one [half], comadre," said his brother-in-law.

They took it. They drank it. The brothers-in-law walked down [the trail] just a short distance together. They would go alone for a stretch of the trail. But you see [one of] the brothers-in-law got drunk. He had drunk a strong dose when they parted company. His brother-in-law's house was probably nearby. "Won't you sleep here in my house, brother-in-law. Will you spend the night?" asked [the second] brother-in-law.

"No, brother-in-law, because [my wife], your younger sister, is waiting up, watching the night go by. She doesn't lock the door, she just pushes the door closed for the night. Something might happen to her," said the [first] brother-in-law.

He meant to go on. He meant to arrive home, But he never arrived home. He jumped over the stream. Toč' they call it, in Na Čih. He jumped. He landed on his knees. He landed rolling, "Oh, hell, I guess I'll rest," he said. Then he tried to rest. He fell asleep. He slept soundly. He didn't wake up, not until the devil went and woke him in the evening. He didn't wake up until he felt [his head] being lifted up and jostled.

Then he felt his hair being wetted down. He felt the cold then, it seems. Then, "How come he's burning?" said the spook. He stood back, he moved away because [the man] was burning. The spook was scared because he was burning. "Oh, but why did I get burnt?" said the spook.

He fled this far away, then he returned again. "I'll put [the fire] out with water. I'm going to bring the water in my mouth. I'm going to scoop it up in my hands," said the spook. But it was no fire! It was because the man was drunk. The man came to, a little. His hair was wetted down. He pretended not to move. He felt how cold [the spook's] horrible hand was, how [his head] kept being touched and lifted up. He just waited for [the spook] to go away. Then he rushed off home. He went to his house. He arrived home. His house was unlocked. He arrived. "Wife, I'm not at all well. I almost died. Don't you see, the spook would have taken me off if your house weren't unlocked. He was following right behind me." Oh, the spook knocked on the door. He knocked on the boards. He kept picking up the hens. He kept picking up the chickens. He shook the chickens off the peach tree. And the chickens were squawking now. But you see all the chickens flew off. The woman noticed, when it dawned the next day, that the hens were lying about, some of them wounded. The sun set. Maybe it was just at dusk. She finished putting her chickens in her house.

[The spook] looked for the house. He tried to open it. He tried to look in the house on the second night. The same thing happened. But now it was the dog he hit. They had a pig. He came and pulled their pig along. He was going to tie the pig up somewhere else. "But, man, our pig has gone," [she said].

"It probably hasn't gone. It's the disgusting devil who is bothering us. [He'll stop] after the three nights are up. Don't be scared," said the man. "Never mind, if it's just a pig it can be replaced. If it's just a chicken it can be replaced. But if it's me who dies, me who goes, then there will be no one to come prepare the food for your chickens and pigs. But so long as I'm alive, never mind. In the end you'll see." When it dawned after the second night they saw a puddle of blood by the door. Who knows if it was just the dog's blood or what. Their dog was not there at dawn.

You see, the dog had gone to the stile. The dog was curled up there asleep. But one of its ears was hurt. You see it was because [the spook] had cut off its ear. Who knows what use it was to him.

You see, the dog's ear had traveled this far from the stile. The dog's ear was lying there. "It's clear that he's the one who is bothering us, but he'll go. He must have a house somewhere," said the man. On the last night he readied his gun, he readied his stave. He looked to see if [the spook] had arrived. [The spook] arrived, but there wasn't much he could do. He seemed to be looking for chickens. There was only that little hen. Their hen had one chick now. The woman hadn't remembered to collect her eggs. There were two. [The spook sucked them], drank them up.

He left. He left when the three nights were up. "Stay there, you bastard. You don't want company, you don't want to talk [to me]," [the spook] said. He left. The three nights were up. "Forget it," [the spook said].

I don't know if it was three or four months later when he came back again. They went outside [to go to the bathroom]. We go outside late at night, it seems.

That little boy said, "Mother, come feel what it is. A horrible freezing hand is touching my back. Go see what it is," he said.

"How could it be, stupid!" she said. The mother was carrying a torch, but the mother came [back]. It wasn't anywhere. She didn't see anything. But you see, something that looked the size of a cat went inside the house. But it was that spook.

Then they saw him. He was big when he was inside the house. He was big. His hat was big. Only his horrible face was black. "Oh why did you open the house and let [the spook] come in?" said [the man]. Never mind, don't worry. I'll get him out. I'll send off a bullet. You'll see!" the man said. Quickly he loaded his gun. [The spook] was going around inside the house. He loaded his gun. He fired at him. [The spook] was impaled on a pole at the door. He grabbed that pole by the door and stumbled out. That horrible spook was terribly scared. He fled away. But he frightened that little boy. "Mother, a devil caught me. I don't know what it is. A freezing cold hand is touching me," he said .

[The spook] left. The time was up. He arrived to scare them, but at particular times. He didn't arrive every day anymore. He longed to carry off one of the people for company perhaps, because I think he hadn't any friends.

He left. He picked himself up and left. Two months later [the man's] compadre arrived. "I just don't know what to do, compadre. A devil went and kept chasing me at Toč'," he said.

"But didn't he do anything to you?" [the other asked].

"It was still hard for me to escape from [the spook] at Toč'. It was still hard for me to come back. At least I remembered the way home. I came to, it seems, when he kept lifting my head. 'Brother-in-law, brother-in-law,' he said to me when he was wetting my hair.

"I thought it was you. I thought he said brother-in-law, but then I heard he was saying 'brudder-in-law'. So then it became clear. I knew it wasn't you. I had thought it was you who went to wake me," he said.

"Oh no, for I just barely arrived myself. I had a hard time finding the door. I just fell there at the door myself," that brother-in-law replied. "Damn, but why [do you let it happen]? Don't you have a cure for it? Ask for holy water in the church. Put holy water at each corner of the house. Put holy water at the door together with 'older brother' as they call it. Spray the four corners of your house. You'll see, then he won't come," his brother-in-law said. So that's what he did. [The spook] didn't arrive anymore. So that's the way it was left till now.

Now we are brave if there is "older brother." Whoever knows how to grind "older brother." Do you know what "older brother" is? It's tobacco, well ground, well prepared. That's "older brother." "Remember 'older brother,' remember to put it at your door. Let it guard your door," said his brother-in-law.

"I've already put it there," he said.

"Take care, take care of yourself."

"All right, brother-in-law."

"We'll talk together tomorrow. Take care of yourself. We'll see how you get through the night," he said.

"OK," he said.

You see, it was the last time [the spook] came. He didn't come anymore when they protected themselves. Because [tobacco] is a protection, it's even a protection against assassins. (RML, tale 127)

THE MAN WHO TOOK THE SPOOK'S WINGS

Once there was a man who went to the lowlands. He was returning from the lowlands. He had many mules. He unloaded them halfway up the mountain. He piled up all his packs there halfway up the mountain where he [was going to] sleep.

The man slept. And he ate contentedly before he went to bed.

Now that night was coming he got very scared. He shook. He was quaking now terribly.

"God, my Lord, what's going to happen to me later on tonight?" he said.

He had a gun. Well, he ate a lot before going to bed. He slept. He slept in the midst of his packs. He laid his gun down at his side when he went to bed.

Because he was tired he fell asleep. He slept. And when he woke up there was a spook squatting there at the fireside eating. He had put aside some leftover beans for the night, thinking he would eat them the next day. When he woke up, the spook was having a good meal. He was squatting and eating happily.

"Oh, no! But what can I do about that?" he said. And quickly he picked up his gun. Quickly he sent bullets whizzing after him.

The spook's chest was well-peppered with bullets. Oh, the spook flew off now. He went to the other side of the mountain. The moon was very bright. It was light. The man had seen where the spook landed.

When dawn came he went to look. He took up his gun. He went, went to look. [The spook] was squatting in a gully. Squatting there in the gully, the spook was bandaging his chest.

When the man arrived carrying his gun, "Oh, don't kill me!" said the spook. "Don't do that. I've already been hit, but look at the size of the bullet wounds," he said.

"What a bastard! Why shouldn't you be shot, bastard! Why did you come scaring me at night time? What are you looking for?" said the man.

"Well, if you want [me] to, I'll give you lots of money, but not if you mean to kill me. Only if you let me go free, then I'll give you lots of money," [the spook] said.

"Well, give it to me then, as much money as you want. Give it to me. Then I surely won't kill you," said the man. He was given money. He was given lots of money. The spook gave it [to him]. First [the man] took the money and then he sent bullets whizzing after him again. He peppered him with bullets again.

[The spook] died. Then [the man] cut the spook into little pieces.

He looked at him, turned him over, turned him around. There was something on his heels. "What could that be?" he said. "Could that be his flying apparatus?" said the man. He took the things off his heels, the spook's flying apparatus it seems. He stuck them on his [own] heels too. And then he stuck them on his heels . . . since maybe he wanted to go look where the home of the spook's wings was, wanted to return them to their home.

The man stuck them on his heels. Maybe he thought it was a good [idea]. Now when he finished sticking them on his heels, one after another, he flew. Gliding off now, he left. It was the spook's wings that carried him away, it seems. He left. He arrived in Guatemala.

"What are you looking for?" said the people there in Guatemala.

"I'm not looking for anything. It happened like this and this. A spook went and scared me a bit. I don't know why," he said.

"Oh but that one, you see, he left in a hurry. But I saw him. He was standing here just at dusk," said the people there.

"I certainly don't know. I saw him like [I told you]. He went and scared me," said the man. "That's why I killed him," he said.

"Go then!" said the people. "Go! Now you have your money. You [can] return, you [can] go enter your house," they said.

Well, the man was elated now that he got lots of money. On and on he came. He came from very far. "Well, I'll let everyone know what the spook is like, how far [the wings] carried me," he said.

Well, he came. He returned home. There wasn't any trouble at all. He just returned to show his money. Well, he returned to tell his children what had happened to him. "The spook did this and this and this to me," he said when he returned.

Well, that's the way it was. They still talk about it, about how it is true that a man once hit the spook with bullets. That's why it was left that way. He told his children about it. That's why [it has been handed down] 'til today just like that.   (RML, tale 125)

Black-man Asks for Children

Once the spook prayed to Our Lord. "Won't you give me permission? I want several of your children," he told St. Lawrence.

"I won't ever give away my children. Why don't you go talk to John. See if he'll give you his," said St. Lawrence.

Well, as for John, "Okay," he said. "Look for them, look!" St. John gave permission. John is his name. [That's what] John said.

"Larry doesn't want to give them away, he doesn't want to give his children. Nothing doing. I went to talk to him already, but he won't give them away. Will you kindly give me your children, give me a few?" said the spook.

"Look, look wherever you can find them, look, take them!" the spook was told.

"Not Larry, he's too mean-hearted. He doesn't want to give his. He doesn't want to give even one. I had longed for his children, but he won't give away even one of them. It's because he's so mean-hearted," said the spook.

"Ah no, as for me, I'll give you permission. See where you can get them!" It was because St. John is good-hearted. He gave away his children.

It's just the same now. That's why they can die any time. Now we, not even one of us dies from assassins or whatever, from spooks or whatever. We never die from that. The [people of] Zinacantan center aren't killed by assassins, nor are they ever killed by spooks. But the Chamulas are killed by assassins. They are killed by spooks or whatever, because long ago Our Lord gave permission. That's why it's like it is 'til now. Whenever there are assassins, then it's the Chamulas who die. A few of them die when they are held up or from whatever it is that they die, because it was promised that they could [be taken]. Their saint said so. He gave permission for one or two of his children to die. They could [be taken]. "There are too many," he said. "You can take a bunch of them, there are still too many," said Our Lord.

But St. Lawrence, he didn't give any away at all. "I won't give them, I haven't many children," he said. "There aren't many. Go

talk to John, maybe he'll give you his. He has more children," said
St. Lawrence.

[The spook] went to talk to [St. John]. "Well, okay, you can
take a few," said St. John.

"Well, then, that's fine if you'll be so kind. But Larry is too mean.
He wouldn't give me even one," said the spook. That's the way it
was.   (RML, tale 68)

I DREAM OF THE SPOOK (*Hʔik'al*)

There was a spook there inside Marian K'obyoš's yard. A rock
was standing there. There was a rock there. There was a spring
there. The water was very clear.

"Why would there be a spring there? Why is there a spring
there?" I said to myself.

"Ah, we certainly can't go there. The spook's house is there," I
was told by whoever it was who seemed to speak to me.

"Ah," I said.

As for me, I went to peek at it. But you see, there was a horrible
big buzzard there. It came flapping towards me. It went chasing
after me. But now it didn't look like a buzzard. It was a horrible
person. It was huge, but it was black all over. It went chasing after
me. I ran away. I went home. I ran. Yes!

"What could it mean?" I said to myself.

"Ah, maybe it's persecution [by witchcraft]. Or maybe you'll die,
because you went westwards," my mother told me. Yes!

"Maybe it's dangerous," I said to myself. Yes! "Maybe it's because the place there is dangerous," I said to myself.

There above the agave I saw it. That horrible buzzard returned.
Yes! And it had been big when it went chasing after me. When it
reached the place where the spring was, it was very little. It seemed
like a buzzard then. It had been big. It had looked like a person.
Yes! It was black all over. It grew small when it returned, when it
reached the place at the foot of the rock. Then it entered a split in
the rock. Yes! It stayed there. I had gone to draw water at the foot of
the rock there in the yard that Marian K'obyoš had bought. Yes!

                                                   (RML, dream 190)

APPENDIX IV: Additional Spook Tales Mentioned in Text

A. Tales appearing in the text:

    1. Carnero-woman from Panajachel (Sol Tax 1950: 2560) (Ch. 5)
    2. Man Who Was Turned into a Dog (RML, tale 4)   (Ch. 5)
    3. A Sorcery Story (Thompson 1930: 158)   (Ch. 5)
    4. The Charcoal-cruncher (RML, tale 60)   (Ch. 5)
    5. Xtabai story (Thompson 1930: 157)   (Ch. 6)

B. Tales mentioned but not included here appear in the original version of this paper, a Radcliffe honors thesis, which is deposited in the office of Professor Evon Z. Vogt, Harvard University:

    1. Alferez Becomes a Black-man (Bricker x072)
    2. The Charcoal-cruncher (Bricker 106 x075)
    3. The Charcoal-eater (RML, tale 12)
    4. Carbon-eater (RML, tale 47)
    5. The Man Who Ate Charcoal (RML, tale 81)
    6. Cemetery Nights (about Corpse-eater) (RML, tale 73)
    7. Split-faced Man (Bricker x042)
    8. Story of White Bundle (Zabala Fieldnotes 1957–1960)
    9. El zopilote y el hombre (RML, tale 42)
   10. Buzzard-man (RML, tale 48)
   11. Journey through Hell (RML, tale 9)
   12. Acatan Creation Myth (Siegal 1943)
   13. Lacandon Creation Myth from Lake Pelja (Cline 1944)
   14. The Flood (RML, tale 55)
   15. The Flood (RML, tale 70)
   16. El cuento de una bruja (Castillo 1965)

BIBLIOGRAPHY

Acheson, Nick
  1962. Ethnozoology of the Zinacantan Indians. Summer Field Work
    Report of the Columbia-Cornell-Harvard-Illinois Summer Field
    Studies Program. Cambridge, Harvard University.
  1962–1963. Unpublished Field Notes. Harvard Chiapas Project,
    Cambridge.
Allen, Glover
  1962. *Bats*. New York, Dover.
Anschuetz, Mary H.
  1966*a*. Unpublished Field Notes on Zinacanteco Midwives. Harvard
    Chiapas Project, Cambridge.
  1966*b*. To Be Born in Zinacantan. Summer Field Work Report of the
    Columbia-Cornell-Harvard-Illinois Summer Field Studies Program.
    Cambridge, Harvard University.
Arciniega, Ricardo Pozas
  1947. Monografía de Chamula. Microfilm Collection of Manuscripts
    on Middle American Cultural Anthropology, No. 15, Chicago, Uni-
    versity of Chicago Library.
Asturias, Miguel
  1967. *Mulata*. New York, Delacorte.
Baer, Philip, and Mary Baer
  1950. Materials of Lacandon Culture of the Petha (Pelha) Region.
    Microfilm Collection of Manuscripts on Middle American Cultural
    Anthropology, no. 28. Chicago, University of Chicago Library.
Bahr, Don
  1961. An Episodic Analysis of Two Zinacanteco Myths. Carnegie Stu-
    dent Seminar Papers, Spring 1961. Harvard University.
Barthel, Thomas
  1966. Mesoamerikanische Fledermausdämonen. *Tribus* 15:101–124.
Beidelman, T. O.
  1963. Witchcraft in Ukaguru. In *Witchcraft and Sorcery in East*

Africa, ed. John Middleton and E. H. Winter. New York, Routledge and Kegan Paul.

Bennett, Charles F.
1967. A Review of Ecological Research in Middle America. *Latin American Research Review* 2, no. 3:3–27.

Berlin, Heinrich
1964. El Glifo 'Zotz Invertido.' Antropológica Historia de Guatemala 16:1–7.

Beyer, Herman
1928. Symbolic Ciphers in the Eyes of Mayan Deities. *Anthropos* 23:35–37.

Bricker, Victoria
1965–1966. Unpublished Field Data. Harvard Chiapas Project, Cambridge.
1968. The Meaning of Laughter in Zinacantan. Ph.D. thesis, Harvard University.

Burridge, K. O. L.
1967. Lévi-Strauss and Myth. In *The Structural Study of Myth and Totemism*, ed. Edmund Leach. Edinburgh, Tavistock Publications.

Butler, Mary
1940. A Pottery Sequence from the Alta Verapaz, Guatemala. In *The Maya and Their Neighbors*. New York, D. Appleton-Century and Co.

Carrera, Antonio G.
1949. Notes on San Juan Chamelco, Alta Verapaz. Microfilm Collection of Manuscripts on Middle American Cultural Anthropology, no. 23. Chicago, University of Chicago Library.

Castillo, Moisés Castillo
1965. *Tres cuentos mayas*. Anales: Instituto Nacional de Antropología e Historia 1964. Mexico City, Secretaría de Educación Pública.

Cline, Howard
1944. Lore and Deities of the Lacandon Indians, Chiapas Mexico. *Journal of American Folklore* 57:107–115.

Collier, Jane (Fishburne)
1960–1963. Unpublished Field Notes and Reports. Harvard Chiapas Project, Cambridge.

De La Fuente, Julio
1961. Notas Sobre el Folklore de los Altos. VIII Mesa Redonda:309–318. Mexico City, San Cristóbal de las Casas.

Dieseldorff, Erwin
    1904. A Clay Vessel with a Picture of a Vampire-headed Deity. U.S. Bureau of American Ethnology, Bulletin 28. Washington, D.C., Government Printing Office.

Dorst, Jean
    1967. *South America and Central America: A Natural History.* New York, Random House.

Douglas, Mary
    1966. *Purity and Danger.* New York, Frederick A. Praeger.
    1967. The Meaning of Myth. In *The Structural Study of Myth and Totemism,* ed. Edmund Leach. London, Tavistock Publications.

Early, John D.
    1965. The Sons of San Lorenzo in Zinacantan. Ph.D. thesis, Harvard University.

Foster, George M.
    1944. Nagualism in Mexico and Guatemala. *Acta Americana* 2:85–103.

Friedel, David
    1965. Fiesta of San Sebastian in Zinacantan. Freshman Seminar on the Maya, vol. 2. Department of Anthropology, Harvard University.

Gann, Thomas
    1915–1917. The Chacchac or Rain Ceremony, as Practiced by the Maya of Southern Yucatan and Northern British Honduras. Proceedings of the Nineteenth International Congress of Americanists, Washington, D.C.

Gates, William, ed.
    1932. *Dresden Codex.* Maya Society Publications, no. 2. Baltimore, The Maya Society.

Goetz, Delia, and Sylvanus G. Morley, eds.
    1950. *Popol Vuh.* Norman, University of Oklahoma Press.

Gossen, Gary
    1965. Chamula Oral Narrative. Unpublished, preliminary Field Report. Harvard Chiapas Project, Cambridge.

Guiteras-Holmes, Calixta
    1946. Informe de Cancuc. Microfilm Collection of Manuscripts on Middle American Cultural Anthropology, no. 8. Chicago, University of Chicago Library.
    1961. *Perils of the Soul.* New York, The Free Press of Glencoe.

Hanzak, J.

1967. *The Pictorial Encyclopedia of Birds*. New York, Crown Publishers.

Herskovitz, Melville J.

1958. *The Myth of the Negro Past*. Boston, Beacon Press.

Horton, Robin

1964. Ritual Man in Africa. *Africa* 34:85–104.

1967a. African Traditional Thought and Western Science. I. *Africa* 37:85–104.

1967b. African Traditional Thought and Western Science. II. *Africa* 37:155–187.

Jakobson, Roman, and Claude Lévi-Strauss

1962. Les chats de Charles Baudelaire. *L'Homme* 2:5–21.

Laughlin, Robert

1962a. El símbolo de la flor en la religión de Zinacantan. In *Estudios de Cultura Maya*, vol. 2. Mexico City, Universidad Nacional Autónoma de México.

1962b. Unpublished Corpus of 132 Zinacanteco Tales. Harvard Chiapas Project, Cambridge.

1962–1963. Unpublished Field Notes. Harvard Chiapas Project, Cambridge.

1963. Through the Looking Glass: Reflections on Zinacantan Courtship and Marriage. Ph.D. thesis, Harvard University.

Leach, Edmund

1961. Two Essays Concerning the Symbolic Representation of Time. In *Rethinking Anthropology*. London, The Athlone Press.

1964. Anthropological Aspects of the Study of Language: Animal Categories and Verbal Abuse. In *New Directions in the Study of Language*, ed. Eric Lenneberg. Cambridge, M.I.T. Press.

1968. *The Structural Study of Myth and Totemism* (ed.). London, Tavistock Publications.

Levin, Ira

1967. *Rosemary's Baby*. New York, Dell Press.

Lévi-Strauss, Claude

1963. *Structural Anthropology*. New York, Basic Books.

1964. *Mythologigues. Le cru et le cuit*. Paris, Plon.

1967. *Mythologigues. Du miel aux cendres*. Paris, Plon.

Lincoln, Jackson Stewart

1945. An Ethnological Study of the Ixil Indians of the Guatemala Highlands. Microfilm Collection of Manuscripts on Middle American Cultural Anthropology, no. 1. Chicago, University of Chicago Library.

Lundell, C. L.
1961. The Flora of Tikal. *Expedition* 3:38–43.

Makemson, Maud
1951. *The Book of the Jaguar Priest: A Translation of the Book of Chilam Balam of Tizimin.* New York, Harry Schuman.

Martín del Campo, Rafael
1961. Contribución a la etnozoología maya de Chiapas. VIII Mesa Redonda:309–318. Mexico City, San Cristóbal de las Casas.

McBryde, Felix Webster
1945. Cultural and Historical Geography of Southwest Guatemala. Institute of Social Anthropology, Smithsonian Institution, no. 4. Washington, D.C., Government Printing Office.

Mendelson, E. M.
1957. Religion and World-view in Santiago Atitlán. Microfilm Collection of Manuscripts on Middle American Cultural Anthropology, no. 52. Chicago, University of Chicago Library.

Miles, S. E.
1957. *The Sixteenth-Century Pokom-Maya: A Documentary Analysis of Social Structure and Archaeological Setting,* vol. 47, part 4. Philadelphia, The American Philosophical Society.

Miller, Wm. Marion
1944. How to Become a Witch. *Journal of American Folklore* 57: 280.

Morley, Sylvanus G.
1938. *The Inscriptions of the Peten,* vol. 3. Washington, Carnegie Institution.
1956. *The Ancient Maya.* Stanford, Stanford University Press.

Nash, Manning
1967. Witchcraft as a Social Process in a Tzeltal Community. In *Magic, Witchcraft and Curing,* ed. John Middleton. New York, The Natural History Press.

Osburne, Lilly de Jongh
1965. *Indian Crafts of Guatemala and El Salvador.* Norman, University of Oklahoma Press.

Paul, Benjamin D.
1962. Ethnographic Materials on San Pedro la Laguna, Sololá, Guatemala. Microfilm Collection of Manuscripts on Middle American

Cultural Anthropology, no. 54. Chicago, University of Chicago
Library.

Propp, V.
    1958. Morphology of the Folktale. Indiana University Research Cen-
    ter, volume 24, number 4:79–105.

Radin, Paul
    1929. Huave Texts. *International Journal of Linguistics* 5:1–56.
    1956. *The Trickster; A Study in American Indian Mythology.* New
    York, Philosophical Library.

Rands, Robert L., and Robert E. Smith
    1965. Pottery of the Guatemalan Highlands. In *Handbook of Middle
    American Indians*, vol. 2, ed. Gordon Willey. Austin, University
    of Texas Press.

Recinos, Adrian, and Delia Goetz, trans.
    1953. *Annals of the Cakchiquels.* Norman, University of Oklahoma
    Press.

Redfield, Robert
    1936. *The Coati and the Ceiba.* Maya Research 3. New Orleans,
    Tulane University.
    1945a. Ethnographic Material on Agua Escondida. Microfilm Col-
    lection of Manuscripts on Middle American Cultural Anthropology,
    no. 3. Chicago, University of Chicago Library.
    1945b. Notes on San Antonio Polopo. Microfilm Collection of Manu-
    scripts on Middle American Cultural Anthropology, no. 4. Chicago,
    University of Chicago Library.

Redfield, Robert, and Alfonso Villa Rojas
    1934. *Chan Kom: A Maya Village.* Washington, Carnegie Institution.

Reichel-Dolmatoff, G.
    1949–1950. Los Kogi: Una tribu de la Sierra Nevada de Sta. Marta,
    Colombia. Revista del Instituto Etnológico Nacional (4). Bogotá,
    Colombia.

Reina, Ruben E.
    1966. *The Law of the Saints: A Pokomam Pueblo and Its Community
    Culture.* New York, Bobbs-Merrill.

Rosales, Juan de Dios
    1949. Notes on San Pedro La Laguna. Microfilm Collection of Manu-
    scripts on Middle American Cultural Anthropology, no. 25. Chi-
    cago, University of Chicago Library.
    1950. Notes on Santiago Chimaltenango. Microfilm Collection of

Manuscripts on Middle American Cultural Anthropology, no. 30. Chicago, University of Chicago Library.

Rosny, Leon de

1887. *Codex Peresianus. Les manuscrits de l'antiquité Yucateque.* Conservé a la Bibliothèque Nationale de Paris. Paris, Au Bureau de la Société Américaine.

Roys, Ralph L.

1931. *The Ethno-Botany of the Maya.* Middle American Research Series, no. 2. New Orleans, Tulane University.

1946–1948. *Book of Chilam Balam of Ixil.* Notes on Middle American Archaeology and Ethnology, vol. 3. Washington.

1965. *Ritual of the Bacabs.* Norman, University of Oklahoma Press.

1967. *Book of Chilam Balam of Chumayel.* Norman, University of Oklahoma Press.

Saler, Benson

1967. Nagual, Witch and Sorcerer in a Quiché Village. In *Magic, Witchcraft and Curing*, ed. John Middleton. New York, The Natural History Press.

Seler, Eduard

1894. Fledermaus-Gott der Maya-Stämme. Zeitschrift für Ethnologie, volume 26. Berlin, Verlag von A. Asher and Co.

1909. The Animal Pictures of the Mexican and Maya Manuscripts. In *The Collected Works of Eduard Seler*, vol. 4, part 5. Cambridge, Peabody Museum Library.

1963. *Codice Borgia*, vol. 3. Mexico City, Fondo de Cultura Económica.

Siegal, Morris

1943. The Creation Myth and Acculturation in Acatán, Guatemala. *Journal of American Folklore* 56:120–126.

Stanek, V. J.

1962. *Pictorial Encyclopedia of the Animal Kingdom.* New York, Crown Publishers.

Starr, Elizabeth

1950. Field Notes on San Andrés Tuxtla. Microfilm Collection of Manuscripts on Middle American Cultural Anthropology, no. 33. University of Chicago Library, Chicago.

Stuart, L. C.

1964. Fauna of Middle America. In *Handbook of Middle American Indians*, vol. 1, ed. Robert West. Austin, University of Texas Press.

Stubblefield, Phil.

    1961. A Study of Some Zinacantan Myths. Carnegie Student Seminar Papers, Spring 1961. Harvard University.

Summers, Montagne

    1928. *The Vampire: His Kith and Kin*. London, Kegan Paul, Trench, Trubner and Co., Ltd.

Tax, Sol

    1947. Notes on Santo Tomás Chichicastenango. Microfilm Collection of Manuscripts on Middle American Cultural Anthropology, no. 16. Chicago, University of Chicago Library.

    1950. Panajachel Field Notes. Microfilm Collection of Manuscripts on Middle American Cultural Anthropology, no. 29. Chicago, University of Chicago Library.

    1959. Folktales in Chichicastenango: An Unsolved Puzzle. *Journal of American Folklore* 62:125–135.

Taylor, Archer

    1956. Raw Head and Bloody Bones. *Journal of American Folklore* 69:114, and 175.

Thompson, J. Eric

    1930. *Ethnology of the Mayas of Southern and Central British Honduras*. Anthropological Series, vol. 17, no. 2. Chicago, Field Museum of Natural History Publication.

    1932. The Humming Bird and the Flower. *The Maya Society Quarterly* 1:120–122.

    1954. *The Rise and Fall of Maya Civilization*. Norman, University of Oklahoma Press.

    1962. *A Catalogue of Maya Hieroglyphs*. Norman, University of Oklahoma Press.

    1966. Maya Hieroglyphs of the Bat as Metamorphograms. *Man* 2: 176–184.

Thompson, Stith

    1955. Myths and Folktales. *Journal of American Folklore* 68:482–488.

Tozzer, Alfred M., ed. and trans.

    1941. Landa's relación de las Cosas de Yucatán. Peabody Museum Papers, vol. 18. Cambridge, Peabody Museum.

Tumin, M.

    1945. San Luis Julotepeque: A Guatemalan Pueblo. Microfilm Collection of Manuscripts on Middle American Cultural Anthropology, no. 2. Chicago, University of Chicago Library.

Turner, Victor W.

1962. *Chihamba: The White Spirit.* Rhodes Livingstone Paper, no. 31. Manchester, Manchester University Press.

1967. *The Forest of Symbols.* Ithaca, Cornell University Press.

1968. *Drums of Affliction.* London, Oxford University Press and the International African Institute.

Vaillant, George C.

1941. *Codex Borbonicus: A Sacred Almanac of the Aztecs.* Cambridge, Peabody Museum.

Villa Rojas, Alfonso

1946. Notas sobre la etnografía de los indios tzeltzales de Oxchuc. Microfilm Collection of Manuscripts on Middle American Cultural Anthropology, no. 7. Chicago, University of Chicago Library.

Vogt, Evon Z.

1960–1962. Unpublished Field Notes and Interviews. Harvard Chiapas Project, Cambridge.

1964. The Genetic Model and Maya Cultural Development. In *Desarollo Cultural de los Mayas,* ed. Evon Z. Vogt and Albert L. Ruz. Mexico City, Universidad Nacional Autónoma de México.

1965. Zinacanteco 'Souls.' *Man* 29:33–35.

1968. Human Souls and Animal Spirits in Zinacantan. Unpublished paper written for the Lévi-Strauss Festschrift. Harvard Chiapas Project, Cambridge.

1969. Zinacantan: A Maya Community in Highland Chiapas. Cambridge, Harvard University Press.

Volta, Ornella

1962. Le vampire. Bibliothèque International d'Erotologie, no. 8. ed. Jean-Jacques Pauvert. Paris, Tauvert.

Wagner, Philip

1964. Natural Vegetation of Middle America. In *Handbook of Middle American Indians,* vol. 1, ed. Robert West. Austin, University of Texas Press.

Wisdom, Charles

1940. *The Chorti Indians of Guatemala.* Chicago, University of Chicago Press.

Zabala, Manuel T.

1957–1960. Unpublished Field Data. Harvard Chiapas Project, Cambridge.

Subject Index

Acanceh, Mexico: bat symbolism at, 60–61

Acatán, Guatemala: creation myth from, 78

Acheson, Nick: 77–78, 82

adultery. SEE sexual promiscuity

Africa: and anomalous human behavior, 5; anomalous animals in, 75, 78n; human transformations in, 93n

agave: and bats, 64

Agua Escondida, Guatemala: spooks in, 101n; *characotel* and *cadejo* in, 145; *siguanaba* and *sirena* in, 150

air-ground opposition: and spooks, 7; and transforming animals as mediators, 122, 124. SEE ALSO, oppositions

Alfereces: at San Sebastian fiesta, 40; at *karnaval*, 47; importance of, 47n; and *h?ik'aletik* impersonators, 79n; making of *chicha* by, 118n. SEE ALSO officials, public

alive–dead opposition: and spooks, 6, 7, 9, 86, 121; arbitrariness of, 86, 125; and sickness, 92; and Split-faced man, 96; and spooks' victims, 101; ritual as mediator between, 122–124; humans as mediators between, 124. SEE ALSO oppositions

?anhel: and association of bat and rain, 70–71; as euphemism, 70–71, 128–129

animals: and anomalous human behavior, 5; and spooks, 6–7, 8, 145, 146, 148; attachment of spooks' heads to, 7, 94–95; humans-turned-into, 7–8, 143–147; theft of, as substitute for rape, 22; association of *h?ik'al* with, 28, 43; as opposite of humans, 42; and *h?ik'-aletik* impersonators, 42–43, 44; correspondence of, to foreigners, 43; and unrestrained sexuality, 46–47; and Maya buffoons, 51; ambiguity of impersonators of, 52; and witches, 75, 146; permanently becoming, equivalent to death, 95; wives of cargoholders compared to, 133; distinction between humans and, 133–134; spooks as protectors of, 147; humans

who become spooks with characteristics of, 147–150

—, anomalous: defined, 4–5, 75–77; and spooks, 7, 75; and Tzotzil Maya, 69; and bat, 69, 129; at San Sebastian fiesta, 75; and domestic animals, 76; habitat of, 76; and refuse, 76; and humans, 133. SEE ALSO bats; buzzards; chickens; dogs; goats; iguanas; jaguars; mice; monkeys; squirrels

—, domestic: and spooks, 7, 8, 99, 143, 144, 145, 146; and waste, 7, 114, 116; and anomalous animals, 76

—, stuffed: at San Sebastian fiesta, 41, 46, 47, 48, 77–79; as symbols of women, 46, 47; feeding of, 48; and ritual buffoons, 50–52; as anomalous animals, 75

—, transforming: interrelatedness of, 83; as mediator between oppositions, 83–84, 122, 124; and human foetus, 105n–106n; absence of bat among, 129; mentioned, 75, 77. SEE ALSO armadillos; bats; butterflies; buzzards; caterpillars; doves; hummingbirds; mice; opossums; rats; toads

—, wild: as spooks, 143; and *brujos*, 146

animal souls. SEE souls, animal

anomalies: cultural methods of dealing with, 4–5; and social norms, 120–121

armadillos: stuffed, 51; as transforming animals, 69, 81–82, 83, 84, 122; comparison of, to pangolins, 75n; description of, 81–82; and vultures, 81–82, 83, 84, 122; food of, 82; and food taboos, 83 and n.

arrows: as accoutrements of *h?ik'aletik* impersonators, 42; as rain symbol, 53

ashes: and spooks, 91, 93–94; as disambiguating substance, 96; as waste, 116

Asturias, Miguel: on spooks, 145, 150

atole: and human foetus, 114–115, 123. SEE ALSO corn; lime water

auitzotl: and drunkards, 115

119, 120, 131; and vampire, 35n–36n; and bat demon, 37, 57, 58, 72–73, 119, 120; and rain, 53, 67–68; and bats, 55, 58, 63, 64, 68, 69, 70, 77, 84, 119–120, 130–131; and flowers, 62-63, 84; and macaws, 63; and nectar, 63, 64, 66; and butterflies, 63, 84; and hummingbirds, 63, 84, 130, 131; and the soul, 101; and lime, 105; and blackness, 105 and n., 118; and *atole,* 117; and vultures, 130, 131

—, menstrual: and human foetus, 114–115, 122, 123; as waste, 115, 116, 122, 123; and *nixtamal,* 117, 120, 122; dangers of, 122–123. SEE ALSO menstruation

boars, wild: and food taboos, 83

bolometik: animallike behavior of, 42; costumes of, 42, 46; mocking by, 47, 106n; and *hʔikʼaletik,* 53; and stuffed animals, 77, 99; punishment of, 100. SEE ALSO jaguars

Bolom Teʔ: and food, 48; and association of *bolometik* and *hʔikʼaletik,* 53

bombax tree: and flower bats, 64

Bonampak (Chiapas), Mexico: Blackman at, 129n

bones: and *el güin,* 8; as fuel for eternal fires, 115

Book of Chilam Balam of Chumayel: on Kinich Kakmo, 62; and association of bats and flowers, 63–64

brave-cowardly opposition: and *hʔikʼal,* 106–108n. SEE ALSO cowardice; oppositions

bravery: rewards for, 23, 27–28, 107, 113; and mens' roles, 23, 121; in tales, 26–27; and *hʔikʼal,* 106–107, 107–113

bread: and *hʔikʼal's* diets, 30, 34, 36 and n., 48n, 149

Bricker, Victoria: on *hʔikʼal,* 20, 102–103; on fiestas, 40, 50; on anomalous animals, 75–76; on eye-plucking motif, 84; on danger of sleep to *hʔikʼaletik* impersonators, 102; on pregnancy and spoilage, 118n; on Split-faced man, 148

British Honduras. SEE Belize

brujos: activities of, 7, 146; sources for, 139–140. SEE ALSO spooks; witches

buffoons: and stuffed animals, 50, 51–52; and dereliction of duty, 51; and bat demons, 57; and coatis, 77

bull: sacrifice of, at *karnaval,* 105

bulldozers. SEE machines

burros: *characoteles* as, 99. SEE ALSO mules

butterflies: and flying squirrels, 37n; and

hʔikʼal, 37n; and bats, 37n, 73, 84; dead transformed into, 62; and fire, 62, 63, 84; and flowers, 62, 63, 84; and sun, 63; and blood, 63, 84; as transforming animals, 69, 81, 82, 83, 83–84; as *pepenetik,* 80; and hummingbirds, 81, 82, 83–84; and bats, 83; and *okinahual,* 83

"butterfly squirrel": 77–78

buzzard glyph: juxtaposition of, with bat glyph, 59–60

Buzzard-man: and fire, 79, 96n; and *hʔikʼal,* 79, 96n; as transformed human, 79, 96n, 143; sources for, 140; bad smell of, 143; activities of, 146. SEE ALSO spooks

buzzards: and *hʔikʼal,* 28, 33, 36, 69, 79–80, 79n, 90, 130, 131; and bats, 55, 59–60, 63, 73, 84, 130, 131; and sacrifice, 59–60, 63, 84, 84–85, 130, 131; and eye-plucking motif, 60, 63, 84, 130, 131; and sexuality, 66–67, 130 and n., 131; and carrion, 69, 79; and fire, 69, 79, 85; as transforming animal, 69, 79–80, 80n, 81–82, 83, 84, 122, 131; and mice, 79; as anomalous animals, 79–80; and bad odors, 79–80, 85, 87, 130n, 146, 147; and armadillos, 81–82, 83, 84, 122; and food taboos, 83; and hummingbirds, 84; and punishment, 84–85, 131; and laziness, 85, 87; and human consumption of corpses, 87, 88; and disappearance of bat demon from Tzotzil mythology, 130; and blood, 130, 131; and illegitimacy, 131; association of ancient and contemporary, 131; and spooks, 144–145, 146, 147; *lab* as, 145

cacti: and flower bats, 64

cadejo: and domestic animals, 8, 143, 145; and drunks, 101, 145; sources for, 140; and *characotel,* 144, 145; and crosses, 145; hair of, 145; and jaguars, 145. SEE ALSO spooks

Cakchiquel (Indians): and bat, 58, 61; *caok* in, 60

calabash tree: and bats and sacrifice, 64

Camazotz: in the *Popol Vuh,* 60; and association of bats and flowers, 64; and *hʔikʼal,* 71–72, 119n. SEE ALSO bat demon

camphor ointment: in childbirth, 116

cannibalism: as anomalous behavior, 5; and *hʔikʼal,* 19–20, 22, 32, 35, 69, 79, 90, 115n; and *hʔikʼaletik* impersonators, 41, 43, 44; and Skeleton-

37n; and bats, 37n, 77–78; as impersonator's accoutrements, 46, 47, 76, 77,
100; as representatives of women, 47,
100; as anomalous animals, 69, 76, 77;
African folktale about, 78n; *lab* as,
145
storms: and bats, 57, 60
Strong-hand: and *hʔikʼal*, 119
structuralism: 6, 86
Suchitepequez, Guatemala: and *characotel*, 144
sugar: in *karnaval* food exchanges, 48
sun: and sacrifice, 37, 62; in cosmic struggle, 38–39, 148; and bats, 61–62, 63,
66, 73; association of, with Kinich
Kakmo, 62; and flowers, 62–63; and
butterflies, 63; and macaws, 63; and
hummingbirds, 63, 66, 71, 72, 84; and
bat glyph, 71; and disappearance of
bat demon from Tzotzil mythology,
130; and *hʔikʼal*, 148. SEE ALSO
chultotic; light
"sun-face-fire-macaw": 62
sun glyph: and bat glyph, 61; and flowers,
66
supernatural: and *hʔikʼal*, 28
symbols: nonstatic nature of, 37, 57; complexity of meanings of, 57

taboos: about incest, 43n; concerning
food, 83 and n., 118–119, 120; concerning women, 104–105, 118–119,
122–123; about corpses, 105
tails: as accoutrements of spooks, 143,
150
tamales: 114
tapirs: as spooks, 143
Tax, Sol: on ritual buffoons, 50
"tearer-off-of-heads." SEE bat demon
Tentación: 92. SEE ALSO devil, the
tʼen tʼen drum. SEE drums
Teotihuacan: plumed serpent at, 53
theft: and spooks, 8; and *hʔikʼal*, 20, 30,
31, 68, 149; and *hʔikʼal* and bat, 68;
and *characotel*, 144; and *lechura*, 145
Thompson, J. Eric: on relevance of ancient material, 56; on vampire bat, 58;
on *zotz–tzots*, 58; and association of
bat with death, 58–59, 64; on association of bat god with rain, 60–61; on
cauac glyph, 61; on inverted bat glyph,
61; and association of bat with blood,
64; on association of flowers and bats,
64; on association of hummingbirds
and eroticism, 66; on association of
sun and flowers, 66; on eroticism of
vulture, 66, 130n
thornbush: and *hʔikʼal*, 103

tigers: as spooks, 143. SEE ALSO jaguars
Tizimin, Yucatán: and association of bats
and flowers, 63–64; and bat demon,
119
Tlacatzinacantli: and sacrifice, 59; and
eye-plucking motif, 60. SEE ALSO bat
demon
Tlalocs: and association of bats and rain,
60–61
Tlatilco: and Split-faced man, 96
toads: and human foetus, 105n, 122; as
transforming animals, 122
tobacco: and spooks, 91; and *hʔikʼal*, 91,
107; in ritual following death, 92; as
protection for travelers, 93; and Split-
faced man, 96, 148; as civilizing agent,
121–122, 134. SEE ALSO cigarettes
torito: 49 and n.
tortillas: as dog food, 8n, 88; and *hʔikʼal*,
30, 33, 36 and n., 149; and *hʔikʼaletik*
impersonators, 48 and n.; and *chic*, 51;
and civilized behavior, 90; and *nixtamal*, 114; and babies, 114–115, 117;
in Lacandon creation myth, 116; and
women's roles, 117; mentioned, 49
travelers: and spooks, 7, 150; anomalous
nature of, 92–93; and *hʔikʼal*, 102, 106,
107
trees: raising ceremonies of, 77; bats and
bad odors of, 80; and *okinahual*, 83;
in destruction of charcoal-cruncher, 95.
SEE ALSO ceiba tree
tsots. SEE bats
turkey buzzard. SEE buzzards
turkeys: and *hʔikʼaletik*, 25; and armadillos, 83 and n; and Nabaj men, 146;
and *naguales*, 146
Turner, Victor: on ritual, 3, 4n
Tzeltal (language): reputation of *hʔikʼal*
in, 38; and connection between Moors
and *hʔikʼaletik*, 52, 132
Tzinacantli. SEE bat demon
Tzotzil (language): and meaning of *ʔikʼ*,
36, 37; reputation of *hʔikʼal* in, 38;
implications of *kaslan* in, 43; connection between Moors and *hʔikʼaletik* in,
52; relation of, to ancient Maya, 56;
mentioned, 40
Tzotzil Maya: and spooks, 6; types of
Black-men among, 19; origin of beliefs
about *hʔikʼaletik* among, 52–54; association of flowers with sacrifice among,
62–63; and anomalous animals, 69;
fear of Negroes by, 72; mentioned, 9.
SEE ALSO Maya
Tzotzil uinic: bat worship by, 58

ʼuch. SEE opossums

Index of Foreign Words Occurring in Text